Say Goodbye to Crazy

Praise for Say Goodbye to Crazy

From Tom Golden, LCSW, author of The Way Men Heal.

"Paul Elam and Dr. Tara Palmatier have a winner with Say Goodbye to Crazy. The book cuts directly through the haze of pop psychology misinformation and unleashes a torrent of reality and sound thinking on a subject that most fear to even talk about: Abusive, high-conflict ex-wives and girlfriends.

If your current relationship is troubled because she continues to use children, relatives or family courts to inflict pain and suffering then you and your partner both need this book. Highly recommended."

From Peter Lloyd, columnist and author of Stand by Your Manhood.

"Frank, factual and full of inconvenient truths."

From Erin Pizzey, founder of the women's shelter movement, expert on domestic violence and author several books, including Prone to Violence and This Way to the Revolution.

"If you have a "Crazy' in your life this is the book for you. Dr. Palmatier and Mr. Elam teach you sound, practical strategies to survive "Crazy" and may well save not only your sanity, your relationships with your partner and children but also your life."

From Barbara Kay, columnist for the National Post.

"As a journalist who writes frequently about gendered imbalances in the family law system, I have received hundreds of anguished personal narratives from loving fathers who have been targeted for alienation from their children by vengeful ex-wives.

Sometimes I hear from the extraordinary women – new partners - who love these men and their children, but did not realize their new relationship came with wearyingly heavy baggage: namely, the unwanted, but ongoing presence in their household of the woman I recognize from these pages as "Crazy."

In this briskly straightforward, vigorously drawn portrait of Crazy, the authorities and ideologues that abet her, and the collateral damage they cause together, authors Palmatier and Elam bring a powerful light to bear on a common, but insufficiently understood post-breakup malignancy. This is a book that will be gratefully received by Crazy's adult victims, but if it is to be effective in ending the child abuse Crazy is responsible for, it should also be read by every family court judge in America."

Suzanne Venker, author and FOX NEWS analyst.

"Sometimes you need a psychologist who will sit and listen. Other times you need one who tells the truth. When it comes to crazy exes, only the latter will do."

Helen Smith, PhD, forensic psychologist and author of Men on Strike.

"If you have an ex-wife in your life that is ruining your current marriage and wreaking havoc with your family, read this book. It will give you the answers you need to live a life free of chaos, anger and frustration. Say Goodbye to Crazy is one of the few books that addresses how to cope with a hostile, angry ex-wife whose destructive behavior is overlooked by the courts, the society and sometimes, even your own husband. It is a life-saver."

Robert Franklin, attorney, family court reform activist, and Board Member of the National Parents Organization.

"Married to a someone with Borderline Personality Disorder? Divorced from one? Are her problems yours even though you're divorced? Will she not let go? Is she abusive? Does she use the kids as weapons against you? Have her issues become your issues, preventing you from having a healthy relationship with your new love? Are your kids becoming more alienated from you by the day? Then the woman you married was Crazy. The woman from whom you're divorced is Crazy, too. In Dr. Tara Palmatier's and Paul Elam's new book, "Say Goodbye to Crazy," the authors teach men reeling from divorce how to spot Crazy and how to deal constructively with her love of control and conflict. Those men won't get this information anywhere else. It's a must-read for men in a relationship with Crazy."

Say Goodbye to Crazy

How to Get Rid of His Crazy Ex
and Restore Sanity to Your Life

Dr. Tara Palmatier, PsyD & Paul Elam

Table of Contents

Introduction..9

About This Book..15

Part One: Defining the Problem 19

1. Normal Divorce Bitterness vs. Crazy Divorce Bitterness 20

2. What Makes Crazy Crazy: The Fearsome Foursome 28

3. High-Conflict People: Crazy by Any Other Name Is
   Still Crazy..38

4. Personality Disorders: You Can't Argue with a Sick Mind 47

5. The Golden Uterus..57

6. Lie Down with Crazy, Wake Up with Fleas...........................64

7. Parental Alienation Syndrome:Brainwashing and
   Weaponizing Children...69

8. Pointing a Crooked Finger: How Crazy Uses the Power
   of Lies to Abuse and Control Victims 77

9. Compassion for Crazy: or, Sympathy for the Devil.................82

10. The Dangers of Labeling Crazy "Crazy"..............................85

11. Gurus, Enablers, and Apologists 89

Part Two: Preparing to Solve the Problem 95

12. Are You Ready to Change?...97

13. Getting on the Same Page...102

14. Obstacles to Saying Goodbye to Crazy 110

15. A Letter to Husbands and Boyfriends...............................117

16. A Letter to Wives and Girlfriends 124

17. Daddy Guilt: Divorce Means Having to Say You're Sorry Forever 132

18. Stepmom Guilt: This Ain't the Brady Bunch....................137

19. The Theory and Practice of Bringing the Pain.....................145

20. Solutions: This Stuff is Hard...152

Part Three : Solving the Problem **159**

21. Putting on Your War Paint..160

22. The Contract Crazy Doesn't Get to Sign, But You Do! 165

23. Identifying and Using Crazy's Fears to Protect Yourself.......168

24. Safety First: Assessing the Threat Crazy Poses and Your Vulnerabilities 176

25. Crazy-Proofing and Crazy-Busting......................................181

26. Boundaries: Why We Don't Negotiate with Emotional Terrorists..187

27. Setting Boundaries with Alienated Children........................194

28. The Three D's: Detach, Disengage, Defend 203

29. Parallel Parenting: Because You Cannot Co-Parent with Crazy 211

30. Communication: Less is More 216

31. Know Thy Custody Order..225

32. Getting Back on the Horse...233

33. Guidelines for Seeking Professional Help 240

34. Face-to-Face Interactions..245

35. Redefining Winning...252

References...259

Introduction

Meet Crazy

Who is Crazy? Well, if you plunked down your hard-earned money to buy this book, you're probably already well acquainted with her. In fact, you're likely more familiar with Crazy than you ever wanted to be.

In case there's any doubt, Crazy is an ex who is unwilling or incapable of letting go of her former partner and does her level best to continue to control and interfere with his life. Crazy comes in both sexes, male and female, but we decided to focus on the female version of Crazy because so few people do. For many reasons, our culture and the mental health profession do a poor job of addressing the problem of female Crazy. There will be much more about that in the pages ahead, but for now let's just focus on identifying Crazy.

If your husband was once married to Crazy, there are probably times when it seems like she is committed to making his life—and yours—a living hell. She demeaned, exploited and abused your husband while they were together, and she continues to harass him through their shared children and the family court system since their divorce.

Crazy is often very entitled. She acts as if she is owed the sun and the moon and everything in between just because she was once married to and bred with your husband. When trying to describe Crazy and her antics to your family, friends, attorney or therapist, you probably find yourself using words and phrases like controlling, bully, entitled, self-obsessed, hypocrite, liar, hateful, terrorist, vampire, bitch, Jekyll and Hyde, psycho bitch from hell, personality disordered, stalker, whack job and, well, crazy.

Crazy may have taught your husband's children to hate and mistrust him or to see him as a disposable wallet and doormat. She trash talks you to their kids, his family, mutual friends and anyone else who will listen. She may even encourage your stepchildren to be disrespectful to you and to resent your very presence in their father's life and theirs'. If your husband has failed to set healthy boundaries with Crazy, you are probably frustrated by having to deal with the consequences. Perhaps you have been hurt by his hesitance to act decisively to protect his family, even when it is so obviously needed.

At one time or another, you've likely sought either individual or couples counseling due to Crazy's behavior, its impact on you and your family and possibly your husband's inability to do anything about it. Therapists, clergy or friends to whom you have turned for support may have told you that you need to respect Crazy as the mother of their children, that you need to be patient and tolerant of Crazy's ongoing abuse for the sake of the children or that you knew what you were getting into marrying a man with kids.

We are not going to tell you that.

In fact, we are going to tell you the opposite.

Crazy is a pandemic. There are men and women living similar lives of quiet and not so quiet desperation, just like you and your husband. Indeed, if you are reading this, it is very likely that a great deal of your life has already been disrupted, consumed by chaos and disharmony brought about by Crazy.

You have found out the hard way that your husband's previous struggles, the ones that should have ended with his divorce, have followed him into his relationship with you and are causing turmoil for both of you. If there are children involved, that misery only multiplies.

You're likely to be suffering the effects of this financially, as well as emotionally and psychologically. Crazy, who was irrational and abusive when they were together, has continued her antics long after their relationship "ended," and now you, and possibly your children, have become the targets of her maliciousness.

You may have also learned the hard way that the family courts are her best friend, enabling her to manipulate and use children like pawns, to constantly go after his income, disrupt your plans and otherwise undermine your lives together.

Your life has become as crazy as that crazy woman is. It has become difficult and sometimes impossible for you to do something as simple as having a family holiday without her finding ways to interfere with and sabotage your plans. Often, she will use the kids to achieve this goal. She will interfere with their visitation at the last minute, or create a crisis that you must respond to at the most critical and inconvenient of times. She has elevated troublemaking to an art form, and your home life has become her canvas.

She will demonize you to his children, encouraging them to disrespect you and to see you as the evil stepmother. She will tell them she cannot provide the things they want because their father is spending all his money on you or on your children. She may even tell them that if it were not for you she and their father would be reconciled and be one "happy" family again.

She will also encourage the kids to disrespect him and to see him as the loser she thinks he is. Crazy will alienate the children from their father, withhold them from visitation and encourage them to blame him for their broken family. The results of that type of abuse are heartbreaking.

If most or all of this applies to your life, you are part of a large and growing community of women whose relationships have become the second battleground for his failed relationship with Crazy. It is not what you bargained for in the beginning, but it is what you are getting, and you are more than sick of it.

If you are reading this book, you are probably also frustrated with *him* because he seems either unable or unwilling to do anything about it. You want him to fight to protect you and your relationship, but it just isn't happening. In response to the ongoing abuse, many men learn to shut down and shut it out. Of course, they are really just hiding from conflict in the only way they know how—by withdrawing. That does nothing to solve the problem. His approach to dealing with Crazy didn't work in their marriage, and it is failing again.

You love him, but you have sometimes wondered just how much of this you can take and hold onto your sanity. You may even have considered leaving.

If this is describing your life, the last thing you need is to spend your time looking for answers in a book that does not have them. It's time for real answers, and time to take real-world action.

This book does have answers. Not all of them are pretty. In fact, most of them aren't. But they are real answers to your very real problems. We are betting by now that you are more interested in solutions, in things that *work*, rather than comfortable pop psychology and socially acceptable platitudes that have not worked.

As you read the table of contents, you will see the list of chapters and topics covered in this book, so there is no need to address that here. Instead, let's take a look at what you will not see.

You will not see psychobabble or "self-help" talk. Let us be clear about that from the beginning. You don't need to hear it because you are not the one who is crazy. She is. And we are not here to help her.

You will also not get any advice or suggestions about how to reason with her, change her behavior, make her see the error of her ways or become a better person. In this book, we do not reason or compromise with Crazy, we just find ways to spot it and get rid of it—by whatever means necessary short of a shovel and a roll of duct tape.

We will not encourage you to give her your compassion. If you are dealing with Crazy, compassion is pointless. Any sympathy or understanding you extend will only bring you more difficulty, but you probably already know this.

We will also not be revering Crazy's status as the mother of your husband's children. Crazy is the kind of mother who eats her young and will not hesitate to harm them emotionally, or in extreme cases, physically.

We will not tell you that you need to play handmaiden to your stepchildren or understand how "traumatized" they've been by their parents' divorce and subsequent re-coupling. It is the parents' responsibility to facilitate their children's emotional adjustment and maintain acceptable behavior before, during and after the divorce. It is far more likely that her continued high-conflict behavior is most damaging to the children.

We will not tell you to ignore Crazy's alienation attempts and ignore the lies, half-truths and distortions she feeds the children in the hopes that someday they will see the light. Not only can you set the record straight and still take the high road, it is imperative to the children's well-being and development that you tell them the truth.

We will not tell you, "You knew what you were getting into when you married a divorced man with kids," or that you need to "suck it up and deal." No one should have to live in siege-like conditions because Crazy believes she owns her ex for life and has decided to make him pay. You married the person you love, and your relationship does not stand a fighting chance unless you deal with the diarrhea-prone elephant in the living room, i.e., Crazy.

Chances are you have tried a wide range of potential solutions in your attempts to make the situation more manageable. You have tried to be accommodating, understanding and gracious. On the other end, you may have become so frustrated that you have become hostile and/or reactionary. Neither extreme has worked for you.

Nothing has worked. That is the problem.

With this type of person *nothing ever works*. The only sane option at your disposal is to get her out of your lives as much as possible.

The only thing that works with Crazy is to say goodbye to her once and for all, making sure you don't look back, not even for a second.

We understand that shutting her out completely can be difficult, especially when there are children involved. Difficult, yes, but difficult does not mean impossible. It is possible, if you are willing to hold your ground with her—and with *him*.

Much of your ability to say goodbye to Crazy hinges on your willingness to do it and to do it without compromise. This book will not only give you a way to solve many of the problems associated with Crazy, but will also help you cultivate the resolve to get the job done. We will also show you ways to help him become your partner in making it happen.

What you will find is that the information contained here will do a lot more than just help you rid your life of a crazy ex. It will help you in many other ways, as well. Crazy comes in a variety of packages. Crazy friends, crazy employers, crazy family members, crazy co-workers and just plain crazy people are part of our lives at one time or another.

Who hasn't had to deal with a crazy, destructive relative, friend or colleague? After all, isn't putting up with constant craziness a little bit crazy itself?

In a strange way, craziness from other people is a normal part of life. We all face it to one degree or another, but tolerating bitter, nasty, destructive insanity from an ex-wife or from anyone else is a choice and a very unhealthy one at that.

It's time to reclaim your life. Don't waste another second. Go ahead and get started on the first chapters of this book. Then say goodbye to Crazy—and hello to a happier, more peaceful life.

About This Book

This book is about ridding your life, as much as is possible, of the destructive influence your partner's crazy ex, whom we will refer to by the all-purpose descriptor—Crazy. We know Crazy would likely find this label insulting, but we assume you have called her worse, and with good reason.

As you read this book, you may find yourself eager to share it with your boyfriend or husband. He may also be enthusiastic to begin the process of saying goodbye to Crazy. We suggest you think in those terms from the start. Getting your mate to buy into this difficult process isn't just half the battle; it is nearly all of it. In order for our strategies to work, the two of you must form a united front.

You may, and likely already have, found your loved one dragging his feet or quick to reject possible solutions before either of you even tries them. In that light, reading this book might make him more than a little anxious and upset. This is understandable for a few reasons.

First, it's very common for men who have been in relationships with Crazy to develop trauma symptoms. Reading this book may cause him to relive the abuse he experienced while he was with her. Second, following our suggestions may push him to face fears and discomfort he had long before he met Crazy, and he may resist on those grounds alone.

Third, individuals who have been put in one no-win situation after the next by Crazy often develop a sense of learned helplessness, or the belief that nothing they do or say will be effective, so why bother? They give up and let Crazy run amok. You may even feel this way, too, periodically. Crazy maintains her power by wearing her victims down into compliant doormats over time.

Don't be surprised if your husband or you are initially reluctant to read this book and implement its strategies. If reading it is upsetting, find a pace that is comfortable and support each other while you read it through. From time to time, one or both of you may need to take a break from reading the book if it becomes too overwhelming. That's okay, but schedule a time with yourself and each other to resume reading. The strategies in this book will be ineffective if only one of you is doing the work.

You're both going to need to do some heavy lifting. If one of you starts to feel resentful during this process, it may be that the other is not doing his or her share. Crazy is an army of one. Sane and functional must work together.

This book is grouped into three sections:

- Part One: Defining the Problem
- Part Two: Preparing to Solve the Problem
- Part Three: Solving the Problem

Part I: Defining the Problem

Before you can solve a problem, you need to identify and understand it. Since you are reading this book, we assume your husband's or boyfriend's ex, Crazy, is the problem. You need to know more, however, than the basic and obvious fact that Crazy is crazy.

We will look at normal divorce bitterness vs. Crazy divorce bitterness and what makes Crazy tick. We will discuss common personality types and mental health conditions associated with Crazy. Some are Crazy with entitlement issues. Some are Crazy ragers. Some are waif-like, perennial, professional Crazy victims. Some are Crazy stalkers. Some are mentally ill (personality disordered and/or sociopathic). Some are emotionally stunted Crazy children in adult bodies. Some are Crazy violent. Some are Crazy drama queens. Not all of the characteristics we describe will apply to your Crazy. On the other hand, you may find there is much overlap.

We will also examine how Crazy is enabled on a cultural and personal level.

Part II: Preparing to Solve the Problem

This section explores the common roadblocks you will need to surmount in order to prepare yourself to say goodbye to Crazy. You may be surprised that Crazy is not the biggest obstacle to solving the problem. Oftentimes, the most problematic obstacles are you and your husband. This is good news! While you can't fix Crazy, you *can* change your behaviors and attitudes.

We will examine your husband's reticence to say no to his ex and possibly to his children, to say no to his unfair share of guilt and to examine the societal and familial experiences that may be causing you difficulty in developing and maintaining effective boundaries with Crazy.

Part III: Solving the Problem

This section provides real-world, practical solutions you can implement once you are ready to commit to doing the necessary work. We will walk you through the fundamental attributes, basic skills and mindset necessary to say goodbye to Crazy.

We will show you specific strategies, and ways to maintain your resolve while you execute your plan. We will not kid with you or sugarcoat the fact that it can get rough. Saying goodbye to Crazy, and making it stick can feel like throwing holy water on a vampire. It can be a scary experience. After all, fear is usually the number one reason why people let Crazy get away with her antics.

A big part of the work you're about to undertake means facing and walking through your fears. If you are committed to making it happen, we can show you and your partner not only how to make that a successful experience, but one that will enhance the bond you share and bring more value to your personal relationship with each other.

Let's get started!

Part One

Defining the Problem

You've purchased this book for a reason. You may feel very alone. You may be angry. You may despair of things ever improving. We understand. Being immersed in dealing with a crazy ex can be all-consuming and affect every aspect of your life.

We're here to help you take back your life. The first step to solving any problem, large or small, is to understand the problem as much as possible and to figure out what will change things for the better.

In Part One, we will examine what you've been dealing with (Crazy) and why it's a problem. You may already be well acquainted with some or all of it, but you have probably not seen it presented in a way that takes your feelings and needs into account. You and your spouse are not alone in this anymore, if you choose not to be.

As you read the chapters in Part One, you may feel like you are stepping into a carnival fun house. That's okay. Dealing with Crazy often feels that way. The great thing is that you can step back out of it. You do not have to live in Crazytown anymore.

Chapter 1

Normal Divorce Bitterness vs. Crazy Divorce Bitterness

Bitterness and divorce go together like cookies and milk . . . or matches and gasoline. It is hard to imagine one without the other. It is a time when dreams have gone up in smoke, promises and hearts have been shattered—and emotions run wild. Add lawyers to the mix, and even in the best of circumstances it can make otherwise normal, adjusted adults feel a pulse-pounding lust for vengeance and mayhem. One might say that the hostility and scorn are normal in these circumstances, if only for a while.

Eventually, the healing of the grief process begins and people slowly let go of the pain as they begin to imagine the new lives that lay ahead of them. That is a normal part of the process. As devastating as divorce can be, it is, after all, a new beginning, complete with its own aspirations, hopes and dreams. As much as it is a painful chapter in a person's life, it is ultimately about healing and moving on.

Well, unless you're Crazy.

You see, Crazy does not do normal grief in which anger is an essential—but transient— part of the healing process. Crazy gets angry and stays that way for a long, long time. In fact, it could be said that you are reading this book because an ex-wife or girlfriend was too emotionally unstable to grieve in a healthy way and has been stuck in her anger as surely as if it was quicksand.

To understand this better, let's take a brief look at the grief process as defined by Dr. Elisabeth Kübler-Ross in her book, *On Death and Dying,*[1] a seminal work on the subject of mourning and loss.

Essentially, it works like this: Whenever there is a loss, a divorce, a death or even something much more minor like a lost wallet or purse, we all go through a similar, five-stage process.

- **Shock/Denial.** This is where a person either consciously or unconsciously refuses to accept facts. Think of a person staring a hole in an empty parking spot because they cannot accept that their car has been stolen. It is almost as if they think that if they stare at that empty spot long enough, their car will magically re-appear. Now imagine the disbelief many people feel when surprised by being served divorce papers. Often, they will read every line, over and over, as though looking for the words, "April Fools!" somewhere in the documents.

- **Anger.** This is when it begins to sink in that the car is really gone or that those divorce papers are the real thing. You hear people say things like, "I just wish I could catch the jerk who took my car!" They are no longer looking for their missing vehicle. Instead they want to look for the person who took it, and not just to get their car back. They also want retribution. It is an emotionally volatile situation, but at least they are accepting what has happened. The same is often true when a spouse files divorce papers.

- **Bargaining.** The bargaining stage is an attempt to undo the damage. This is especially true where it concerns serious loss, like a pending death. It will often involve praying to whatever god the affected person believes in—a plea for divine intervention. In other cases, it may involve some form of magical thinking, e.g., a man discovers that his wife has had a string of affairs for the duration of their marriage. First, he is in shock and denies the truth (stage 1), and then he becomes angry. "That bitch!" (stage 2). Next, when the pain starts to set in, he may come up with bargaining thoughts, like "Maybe if I buy her that bigger house and get back in shape, she will quit cheating on me." This is somewhat akin to, "Maybe if I call the police, they will find my car and bring it back to me in time for work tomorrow." In that respect, bargaining can be viewed as a more advanced and sophisticated form of denial.

- **Sadness/Depression.** This difficult stage is where the person begins to experience the true pain of loss. Kübler-Ross also referred to this as "preparatory grieving." It is the beginning of the acceptance of the loss, but with a strong emotional attachment to the lost person or object. It is often a powerful experience, so intense it may cause a person to retreat to previous stages in order to escape the pain.

- **Acceptance.** This is the final stage of grief. It is the place where people can experience the loss with much more emotional detachment and objectivity. In the case of a divorce, it's the place where an individual can remember their former spouse, but without anger or other forms of emotional upheaval or the desire for retribution over things that happened in the past.

This sums up the general process of grief that most normal people will go though, to one degree or another, in reaction to a significant loss, including a divorce. The problem is that Crazy goes through a significantly different process. Whereas normal people go through the stages of grief, feeling and dealing with the shock, anger and sadness on their way to accepting the loss and moving on, Crazy's process goes something like this:

- **Shock/Denial.** In this stage, Crazy is identical to normal people. On getting bad news, like divorce papers, she is in stunned disbelief, refusing to accept that her marriage is about to come to an end.

- **Anger.** In this stage, Crazy is also like normal people, only her anger is much more intense. "That bastard!" becomes, "That bastard, I am going to make him pay! He will never see the kids again! I am going to take everything and ruin his life!"

- **Anger.** Crazy doesn't bargain; Crazy gets revenge. This is where Crazy formulates a plan to get even with the person she is losing and/or pushing away. You see, even if Crazy is the one who initiated the break-up, it is still perceived as an abandonment (we know, we know—it's crazy). Crazy will typically embark upon a scorched-earth policy in all divorce, custody and personal matters, up to and including harming herself and the children (e.g., financially, socially, emotionally and even physically) in order to make her ex pay. Crazy will bite her nose off (and everyone else's) to spite her face.

Crazy heads directly for lawyers and the family courts without hesitation. She also starts poisoning the minds of the children, turning other family members and friends against her spouse (and against each other), all with the vindictive intent of inflicting as much pain as possible on the object of her scorn.

*Crazy may engage in a form of bargaining called a Hoover. A Hoover is when she tries to lure her target back by promising things will change, seducing him with sex, guilt trips (e.g., "Think of the children!" or "I will kill myself if you leave me, and it will be your fault!") or straight up intimidation and bullying (e.g., "I will tell the police you beat me and the kids!") It's called a Hoover because, just like the vacuum cleaner, Crazy tries to suck her victim back into the relationship. If her Hoovering attempts fail, she will quickly revert to more obvious anger.

- **Anger.** Crazy doesn't grieve. Crazy just gets crazier, angrier, needier, more malicious, more prone to crazy accusations and, in especially toxic cases, makes false allegations of abuse to law enforcement. By this point, Crazy has figured out that with her easy use of the female-biased family courts and her position as the Golden Uterus (i.e., the sacrosanct "mother of the children"), she can wield almost limitless destructive power over her victim *and anyone who is close* *to him.* Sound familiar? Crazy knows she can hurt you and does not hesitate to do so.

- **Anger.** Crazy doesn't accept . . . *anything*, not even court orders, settlements and custody arrangements that she agreed to and signed on the dotted line. Crazy reserves the right to change her mind, even when there are binding legal documents and admonishments from a judge. The rules are for everyone else; Crazy is too "special" to abide by the laws that lesser, saner and more ethical people are compelled to follow.

Crazy figured out by stage 4 that she doesn't have to accept anything. By this point, she is in the process of refining and expanding ways to express her unresolved displeasure with and rage at her ex. She has figured out the kids are a useful tool, and she uses them without consideration to the harm she may do. The children will become her hostages, foot soldiers and weapons.

Using the children in this way is nothing new for Crazy. It is likely she was using the children as pawns long before divorce became a possibility. It is the divorce, though, that makes her destructive use of her children more pronounced and malignant. She plays with visitation, child support orders and alimony as if she moves them around on her chessboard to wherever she feels they can do the most damage on her command. She delights in hearing the children start to echo her disapproval of their father, which by now is happening with some regularity.

Typically, there is no end to the Crazy grief process. She will cycle through it forever, even if she manages to ensnare a new victim in the form of a romantic interest. At best, he will only be a minor distraction in her hate-fueled war; at worst, he will become her accomplice, stooge and enabler.

Crazy will not change, which means you and your husband will need to change how you interact with and respond to Crazy if anything is going to get better.

What you need to understand (if you don't already) is that Crazy is *crazy*. You cannot reason with Crazy and you cannot negotiate with Crazy. You cannot out-crazy Crazy. Crazy does not compromise. Crazy does not play fair. Crazy never rests. Crazy never takes a vacation. Think of her as a toxic Energizer Bunny; she just keeps seething and scheming and screeching.

Reasonably healthy people divorce because they want the conflict and problems in their marriage to end. They want to find a place of peace. This is not true of Crazy. She is not interested in peace. Her sole intent is to see your lives in pieces.

Crazy wants the conflict to go on infinitely. If you manage to reach resolution with one issue, she will invent a dozen new ones. Conflict is like an energy drink for Crazy. It is the wind beneath her crazy wings. Conflict is the hook by which she continues to keep her targets engaged and there is probably no low too low to keep it going. This is why we will repeatedly hammer home the importance of setting boundaries with and disengaging from Crazy.

Any connection you have with Crazy makes you vulnerable. When children are involved, that may mean you have to live with some vulnerabilities. However, most of the places in which you are now vulnerable to Crazy can be eliminated or significantly decreased.

So there you have it. Such is the "grief process" for Crazy. It is not like any of this is news to you. You have already been living it, day in and day out. But sometimes it helps people, just a little, to see what they are living put down in words by another person. Sometimes it helps to get some outside confirmation of what you already know, even if it is just confirmation that your husband's ex is abnormal in every sense of the word.

That is the main point, after all. It is important to remember that when you are dealing with someone who is capable of staying angry and destructive about a failed marriage, month after month, year after year and decade after decade, you are not dealing with anything but Crazy.

The monster your partner was with has formally become, through their break-up, a monster to all of you—to him, to you, to his children, to your children. No one seems to be beyond her reach or pardoned from her desire to inflict harm.

This ought to be a hint to you—or a glaring neon sign—that this is not a person with whom you try to reason, fight or out manipulate. Her presence in your life needs to be curtailed as much as possible, with the ultimate goal of taking her out of the picture completely.

The first thing you have to do is assess what kind of person she is. Is she just an embittered ex-wife going through the normal grief process on her way to resolution and finding interests other than your relationship with him, or is she a mentally unstable lunatic, bent on inflicting a lifetime of pain for reasons she no longer even understands?

If the answer to that isn't obvious now, we venture to assume it soon will be.

Takeaways

- Crazy is not capable of navigating a healthy grieving process. She is stuck in anger, most likely permanently.

- There is no one who can help that. Not your partner, you, Crazy's mom, the police—no one. Crazy is stuck because Crazy chooses to be stuck. Because Crazy defends against feeling sad, sorrowful, guilt, shame, etc., she gets stuck in anger because it feels better than the alternatives.

- Because Crazy is crazy and stuck, you and your partner must protect your family from her.

- Crazy is not part of your family. Don't give her a place there.

Chapter 2

What Makes Crazy Crazy: The Fearsome Foursome

Understanding why Crazy is crazy, while intellectually interesting, is unlikely to help you. Whether it was not getting a pony for her 6th birthday, or if she was seriously abused by a parent(s) or if she just had lazy parents who gave in to her tantrums and treated her like a little princess instead of telling her no—it doesn't matter. We don't care why Crazy is crazy and neither should you.

That is for her to figure out with a skilled therapist if or when she ever pulls her head out of her ass. We do, however, need to know how to spot Crazy, so you can protect yourself and your family from her.

Crazy can take many forms: Golden Uterus, control freak, princess, psycho-bitch, toxic woman, borderline, narcissist, high-maintenance woman, waif, witch, bully, emotional terrorist, full-blown sociopath, emotional vampire, blood-sucking tick, high-conflict person, personality disordered individual and professional victim. Oftentimes, Crazy will exhibit characteristics from more than one category. No matter what kind of Crazy you have in your life, there seem to be four underlying components that drive and fuel Crazy, or what we call the Fearsome Foursome.

The Fearsome Foursome is comprised of:

- Victim Identity.
- Entitlement.
- Control Freakery.
- Emotional Reasoning.

Victim Identity

There are victims and then there are *professional victims.* Crazy is a lifelong, card-carrying member of the Sisterhood of Professional Victimhood. A true victim does not relish the role of victim. They do not want to be perceived as victims, and they will do whatever they need to do to heal, adapt and move forward in their lives. They do not want to be defined by the harm that was done to them once upon a time.

Crazy, on the other hand, basks in her "victimhood." Of course, her "victimhood" is often of her own making and completely fictional. Establishing a victim identity is how Crazy gains sympathy, attention and other resources. It is also how she wields power.

Crazy may use her elective victim status as a form of social currency and personal power. For example, Crazy plays victim to obtain an ex parte restraining order based on false allegations to punish her ex and gain a tactical advantage in family court. She gets the direct benefit of the protection of the court and law enforcement and punishes her ex by causing him to spend money to defend himself. She may also have him removed from the marital home, separated from their children and possibly damage his career and reputation. Additionally, she becomes eligible for state and federal victim services and monies and gets support and sympathy from people gullible enough to buy her victim act.

Playing victim can help Crazy manipulate and control others by holding them hostage through guilt and obligation. Crazy has no qualms about using guilt and pity to obtain special privileges and favors or to keep a partner mired in a relationship with her. In extreme cases, Crazy will use her victim status to keep her adolescent and adult children tethered to her. Some forms of Crazy see normal childhood development, such as age appropriate autonomy and increasing independence, as her children "abandoning" her.

Playing victim also enables her to mask and/or rationalize her own aggression and abusive behavior. She can't possibly be the aggressor if others see her as the victim, right? If she is overtly abusive, well, she is just acting out of fear because she has been "abused." She can't work and needs more money because she "sacrificed" her career (often against her ex's wishes).

More often than not, Crazy is no victim. She is the aggressor, the classic she-wolf in sheep's clothing. Unfortunately for Crazy's victims, she is adept at flipping situations so that she appears to be the victim of the person she is victimizing. This is an actual psychological phenomenon called DARVO (Deny, Attack and Reverse Victim and Offender).[2] [3]

If you want to be accused of "victimizing" Crazy:

- Call her on her crap.
- Tell her no.
- Stop letting her abuse you.
- Erect and enforce boundaries.
- Deliver natural consequences for her bad behaviors.

To the unsuspecting observer, such as a teacher, coach, custody evaluator, attorney, police officer on a domestic dispute call or rape allegation, friend or judge, Crazy's claims of victimhood, moral outrage and tears may appear real. Most people reason that if she's so upset, something really bad must have happened. Crazy counts on people making this fundamental attribution error.

The tears, anger and fear are often real, but very misleading. Crazy is so desperate to get her way that she works herself into a very convincing tizzy and begins to believe her own lies, and thus becomes even more convincing.

Crazy's victim identity also feeds into and is fed by her sense of entitlement. It fuels her "the world owes me because I am special and because I have been wronged" attitude.

Entitlement

"I am special! Why? Because! It is your job to take care of me. I sacrificed my career to take care of your children. It is your job to support me and <u>my</u> children. I deserve . . . I am entitled to . . . You owe me!"

Narcissism is on the rise in Western culture and Crazy is leading the way.[4] Crazy believes she deserves privileges, exemptions, honors, deference, status and consideration not because she has done anything to earn them, but because she is "special," a mother (the bearer of the Golden Uterus) or because she is a "victim." It is Crazy's gross sense of entitlement that drives the double standards, lack of accountability, lack of empathy (i.e., Crazy's suffering is more painful and more important than anyone else's), lifelong pattern of blame and projection, convenient relative morality and her "you owe me" attitude.

Entitlement is why Crazy believes she can choose which court orders she wants to follow. She fancies herself above the rules and frequently above the law. A sense of entitlement is why Crazy believes that a grown woman should not have to work to support herself and why she should not have to contribute to the children's financial support in any meaningful way. This is particularly evident in Crazy's hostile dependency[5] on her ex, your husband. Specifically, it is what allows her to take money from a person she hates, showing a fundamental lack of integrity, while pretending she is strong and independent.

Crazy is often hateful to and contemptuous of your husband who is forced by the courts to subsidize her choice to be unemployed or underemployed. Crazy will snarl that she does not need her ex and that the children do not need their father, but heaven forbid if her support check arrives a minute late. Crazy will often refer to her ex as a deadbeat, even when his support checks are on time or early. It seems to us that the actual deadbeat is the person who willfully refuses to work and doesn't financially contribute to the care of her children.

Entitlement is why Crazy sees the children's father as an object of utility and a wallet. Because that is how she views your husband, she expects the children to follow suit. Because she lacks empathy for anyone except herself (when you are pathologically entitled, the only person who matters is *you*) she refuses to acknowledge the very important role a loving and involved father plays in his children's life. It is why Crazy puts her own needs, wants and feelings ahead of the children's needs, wants and feelings. Entitlement is what drives Crazy's fundamental selfishness, self-centeredness and solipsism.

Entitlement is especially evident in the self-anointed princesses, queens, divas and Golden Uteri varieties of Crazy. If your husband shares children with Crazy, you have undoubtedly encountered the Golden Uterus. In fact, the Golden Uterus attitude is so prevalent and problematic that we discuss it in *chapter 5*.

Control Freakery

It is normal to want to have control over oneself and one's life to the fullest extent possible. However, reasonable adults understand that you cannot control everything, especially not other people. You can make requests or try to influence others, but you cannot control them, not really. The only person you can control is yourself.

Crazy has yet to come to this realization. In fact, Crazy often wears herself out trying to control everyone and everything—except for herself and her out-of-control emotions.

Crazy lives in a fragile bubble. By now, you probably recognize that maniacal and determined look in Crazy's eyes, the escalation in communications, threats, demands, name-calling, gamesmanship and victim-speak when you resist her efforts to control you. Crazy defends against anything and anyone that might burst that bubble like reality, logic, reason and facts. This why she invests so much energy trying to control the children, your husband, the courts and anyone else she perceives as a threat to her control.

Crazy not only tries to control other people's actions, but also their feelings, thoughts and perceptions. She wants absolute control. Control freakery is how Crazy (mis)manages her anxiety and safeguards her distorted reality, pathological entitlement and victim identity, which are only able to thrive and survive in the bubble she inhabits.

If Crazy were to really look at herself, her behaviors and the damage she causes, how could she stand herself? It is a matter of ego preservation vs. ego annihilation. In other words, Crazy defends and preserves her false self and false reality at all costs. Anything that threatens her ego must either be controlled or eliminated. You and your husband are a very big threat to Crazy in this respect.

For example, she is a wonderful human being, a wonderful mother, a wonderful wife—just *wonderful*. Your husband is the loser, ogre, cheater, deadbeat or abuser. The divorce didn't have *anything* to do with Crazy and her behavior.

Your husband was having an affair (even if he wasn't). He was having a mid-life crisis (even if he wasn't). He's gay (even if he isn't). He couldn't handle being with such a strong, independent woman (even if she's unemployed and financially dependent on him). Then you arrived, proving he is a desirable mate. Therefore, you are a threat because you jeopardize the false narrative that she tells herself and anyone else who will listen. You also offer her children a compare and contrast, which is another threat to her ego and control.

She views her ability to control you as a matter of her psychological survival. This is compounded by the fact that Crazy believes there is a winner and a loser in every interpersonal interaction. She will fight tooth and nail against being the loser. This is why it is virtually impossible for Crazy to compromise or make concessions, and is also why mediation with Crazy is typically a waste of time and money. If her ex is able to get a fair and equitable divorce and custody settlement, it makes it more difficult for her to sell the victim narrative. Everyone knows bad men and bad dads lose in court.

In order for Crazy to feel she is winning, someone else must lose.[6] Because this is a matter of psychological survival to her, she has to steamroll others in order to avoid feeling helpless. Thomas Schumacher, PhD explains, "To relinquish control is tantamount to being victimized and overwhelmed."[7] Compromise and concession are humiliating defeats. Crazy would rather blow the house up and everything in it than compromise or take personal responsibility— unless there is something in it for her.

Emotional Reasoning

We all engage in emotional reasoning from time to time. We have sore spots that periodically cause us to let our feelings get the better of us, and we react *emotionally* instead of *logically*. This is why healthy individuals take time to reality-test their feelings when they realize their emotional response is disproportionate. In other words, we check our feelings against the facts of whatever has caused us to feel excessively bad, mad or sad. In case you haven't figured it out yet, Crazy doesn't do reality much less reality testing.

Emotional reasoning is the fuel that keeps the Crazy train running. Instead of reality testing, Crazy forces facts to fit her feelings, which often change from day-to-day, hour-to-hour and minute-to-minute. Crazy lives in the permanent present of whatever her immediate feeling state is—regardless of whether there is a basis for it in reality.

There may very well be a reason why Crazy feels the way she feels, but it probably has more to do with unresolved hurts, fears and, quite possibly, pathologies that transpired long before her relationship with your husband. Oftentimes, Crazy is playing out a script from childhood that has nothing to do with present day circumstances.

Emotional reasoning says, "If I feel this way, it must be true." For example:

- Don't remember what really happened because your emotions were too out of control? *Make something up. If it feels right, then it is right. What feels right is what makes you feel good. If the truth makes you feel bad or doesn't fit your script (fit your script-of-the-moment), then it isn't right. Get it?*

- Embarrassed by something you did or said? *Deny it ever happened and blame the person who is causing you to feel bad about yourself. Remember, what feels good is the truth, and what feels bad is the lie.*

- Want to get your way at the expense of someone else? *You deserve it. You're entitled. The person standing in your way hates you, is trying to control you, doesn't understand you, doesn't care about you, isn't making you feel heard, isn't making you feel loved, isn't making you feel special. Tell everyone what a monster he or she is and maybe even have them arrested. After all, they deserve it. Who are they to tell you no or get in your way? You're special.*

- On the verge of losing custody because your abusive behaviors have finally become glaringly apparent to the court? *Make up false abuse allegations or, if you're a full-blown sociopath, murder your kids and stage a half-assed suicide attempt.*[8] *When you come to in the hospital, claim you don't remember what happened. When confronted with the evidence, break down sobbing and say you were so afraid your husband would abuse and molest the children that you had to kill them to protect them.*

Crazy rarely lets pesky little details like the truth, court orders, the rights of others or the law get in her way. Emotional reasoning helps her to justify pretty much anything she does, no matter how abusive or criminal it might be. It fuels the self-perpetuating loop of Crazy's victim identity, entitlement and control freakery.

In a nutshell (pun intended), you now have an understanding of what makes Crazy crazy and keeps the crazy train running. On their own, victim identity, entitlement, control freakery and emotional reasoning would be difficult to manage. Taken together, they are the fearsome foursome and explain why you cannot reason and negotiate with Crazy.

Takeaways

- A gentle reminder from Chapter One—You cannot fix whatever it is that drives Crazy or makes her crazy. No one can.

- The Fearsome Foursome—Victim Identity, Entitlement, Control Freakery and Emotional Reasoning—are powerful forces that drive Crazy. Again, you do not have to understand or fix this.

- The Fearsome Foursome can inspire fear of consequences in those who are Crazy targets. It's okay to be afraid. It's normal and healthy to fear those who are bent on destruction.

- Crazy always, always must win. Not just win, but also make you a loser. And as a loser, Crazy must always take something from you. She must feel you are losing something.

- You cannot negotiate or work with any of the above. You must find a different way to deal with the Crazy in your life. Don't try to fix, negotiate, placate, work with or get along with her. It won't work. The only thing that works is getting away from Crazy and using boundaries to keep her at bay.

Chapter 3

High-Conflict People: Crazy by Any Other Name Is Still Crazy

High-conflict person (HCP) is a term that has been around since the 1980s. Family law attorneys use it to describe the "angry twenty percent"[9] of individuals in divorce and custody disputes with certain characteristics that make it difficult, if not impossible, to resolve conflict in a productive and healthy manner for themselves and their children.[10] These characteristics include rigidity, black and white thinking, poor problem-solving skills, extreme emotional responses, the need for control, emotional immaturity, limited personal insight and a persistent pattern of blaming others for *everything*.

In other words, they are jerks who make everyone around them suffer.

HCP is a politically correct, non-inflammatory euphemism term for Crazy. It is used to describe these people in terms that sound tidy when they are actually destructive and dangerous.

You need to know the term HCP as the Crazy in your life probably enjoys tormenting your husband (and you) by endlessly dragging him back to court for not responding quickly enough to her inappropriate and intrusive text messages or for not paying more child support than the court order stipulates. She may also drag you to court for not making special accommodations for her chaotic life or for not allowing her to manipulate, exploit and steamroll you for however long she desires to do so. That does not mean you have to pretend she is anything less than a human disaster.

You may also need to know this term because you might want to find an attorney experienced with high-conflict cases that has a proven track record of handing Crazy her ass in court, but more on this later.

Let's take a look at some of the attributes of Crazy, euphemistically known as HCP.

Characteristics of HCPs/Crazy

Immaturity. Canadian Family Court Justice and author, Harvey Brownstone, observes the importance and necessity of maturity in co-parenting:

> The major difference between couples who resolve their disputes privately and those who turn to a judge has to do with one overriding characteristic: *maturity*. In the context of a relationship breakdown, being mature means loving your children more than you dislike your ex-partner. Being mature means caring enough about your children that you will force yourself to deal in a civilized way with someone you may hate. Being mature means thinking twice and measuring your words carefully before you shoot your mouth off when you're upset with your ex-partner, especially in front of the children. It means always insulating your children from parental conflict so they know your break-up has nothing to do with them. It means doing what is necessary to make the transition in your children's lives as easy for them as possible. Being mature means putting your children's needs ahead of your own. It means truly understanding and accepting that your children are entitled to love and be loved by *both* of their parents. It means giving your children emotional permission to express and receive that love, even though you and the other parent dislike each other. Being mature means being willing and able to reach compromises so that your children can have peace rather than be caught in a tug of war and conflict of loyalties. Being mature means recognizing that you can be an ex-partner but you are never

going to be an ex-parent. True maturity requires parents to appreciate that children need both parents in their lives, working co-operatively to make the best possible decisions for their upbringing. [11]

Instead of resolving conflict and moving on, the immature, high-conflict Crazy becomes stuck in a pattern of creating conflict then shifting blame in an effort to punish and control her ex, even when it is to her own detriment.

We want you to pay attention to that!

Just stop and consider it for a moment. Crazy is figuratively, and sometimes literally, willing to set a house on fire and let it burn down with herself in it if she thinks others will get burned, too—especially if she does not have to put out the fire herself. She may even return to the scene of the fire afterward looking for survivors to "help."

Now *that's* Crazy.

This is what you are actually dealing with and don't let anyone—not therapists, not judges, not family and friends or so-called Borderline Personality Disorder experts—tell you otherwise. Forgetting that, even for a minute, is not advisable. In fact, it is downright foolish.

We have said it before, and we will say it over and over again. Trying to negotiate with, reason with, placate or assuage Crazy is like trying to bargain with a starving, feral dog over a bone he already has in his mouth. It is remarkably inadvisable to even try.

The issue is not the issue.[12] Crazy has issues, lots and lots of issues, but the stated issue is typically not the *real* issue. The real issues are and always have been her personality and behaviors.

For example, high-conflict Crazy sues her ex for sole custody after the judge awarded equal custody in the original settlement. Crazy files the suit because she claims her ex refuses to co-parent with her. In the complaint, Crazy states the ex *never* returns phone calls, *never* responds to emails and texts, refuses to speak with her at custody exchanges, won't sit with her at children's sporting events, etc. Crazy wants the judge to force her ex to attend weekly therapy with her and force him to "co-parent" with her.

In reality, Crazy's ex is an involved and loving father who is setting boundaries with Crazy who has become increasingly intrusive and controlling since the divorce. He replies only to messages that actually require a response, such as schedule changes or true emergencies, and ignores messages in which Crazy is attention seeking and/or attempting to control his parenting time. He says hello and goodbye at custody exchanges, but will not linger to be cross-examined while Crazy tries to agitate the kids.

Let's be real. Crazy doesn't want to co-parent. She is incapable of it. Co-parenting would mean considering the ex's input, sharing control, being able to compromise and setting aside her petty feelings to do what's in the children's best interests—not exactly Crazy's strong suit.

Crazy was incapable of co-parenting during their marriage and even less capable of it after the divorce. She is reeling from the loss of control the divorce decree represents. If Crazy wrote the dictionary, co-parenting would be defined as, "I have unilateral control. As the father, you are at my beck and call. You will be my on demand ATM and don't you dare think you can move on with your life and recouple." Compromise would be defined as, "You give me everything I want and do everything I say."

The stated issue in the court complaint is not the real issue. The real issue is that Crazy is angry with her ex for enforcing healthy boundaries with her. She is feeling ignored and rejected, and her inner professional victim is *pissed*. Crazy wants unrestricted access to the ex for attention and to continue to bully, manipulate and exploit the ex. In other words, she wants to keep things just like they were when they were still married and before he "abandoned" her. For the record, you don't abandon an adult. You *leave* an adult. You haven't abandoned your kids either. Crazy and the enabling family courts are responsible for your forced separation.

Again, Crazy is not taking the ex to court because he will not co-parent with her. She is taking the ex to court because she wants face time with her ex, and expects the judge to force him to do as she wants—like a 5-year old who runs to her parents to complain that her older sibling won't play with her. Any attention is good attention to Crazy.

It's always someone else's fault. Crazy is a blame shifter extraordinaire. She blames others for everything she feels is wrong in her life. Crazy didn't get a D in Economics because she missed 30% of her classes and performed poorly on exams. She got a D because her professor hates her. Crazy didn't have an extramarital affair because she can't go very long without attention and is compelled to engage in dalliances to bolster her fragile self-esteem. Crazy had an affair because her husband is a workaholic who is never home and doesn't appreciate her—never mind the fact that her husband has to work overtime because she refuses to get a job, is an impulsive binge shopper and went into histrionics because she just had to have the one house they couldn't afford.

Crazy typically goes on the attack and accuses her targets of wrongdoing in an effort to distract others from recognizing the real aggressor or culprit—her. While Crazy makes very noisy, emotionally charged claims about how she has been harmed, others rarely notice her monogrammed dagger stuck in the back of the person she claims has victimized her. It is a twisted sleight of hand.

Crazy is typically very emotional when blaming others. It is her intensity of emotions that makes her so convincing, at least initially. While Crazy is long on emotions she is typically short on substantiated facts and details. The trick is to ignore the intense emotionality of her tales of victimhood and ask specific, concrete questions. As you catch her contradictions and call them out, she will manufacture new accusations and claims or become enraged and accuse you of victimizing her.

Crazy does this to keep the conflict going and the blame directed elsewhere. Rather than admit to her lies, half-truths and exaggerations, which Crazy herself may begin to believe, she will become indignant and threaten to sue attorneys, law enforcement, therapists, judges—whoever is trying to hold her accountable. This is just one way a shrewd attorney can get Crazy to let her mask slip in court.

Now we ask you, do you like the term *high-conflict* to describe this person, or does *Crazy* work well enough for you?

HCPs often meet the criteria for personality disorders, and so does Crazy. Disorders that are typically implicated in high-conflict cases include: Histrionic Personality Disorder, Borderline Personality Disorder, Narcissistic Personality Disorder, Antisocial Personality Disorder, Avoidant Personality Disorder and Paranoid Personality Disorder. We will discuss these disorders in *chapter 4.*

HCPs/Crazy create conflict out of fear and malice. Crazy and HCPs are driven by five fundamental fears, which we will discuss in depth in *chapter 23:*

- The fear of abandonment.
- The fear of feeling or being seen as inferior.
- The fear of loss of resources (e.g., attention, status, money, power, control, career, love, etc.).
- The fear of public exposure of their misdeeds.
- The fear of loss of control.

Crazy fears being abandoned by her children and being seen as the inferior parent, which is why many Crazies engage in parental alienation behaviors and try to block access to the other parent. They also make false allegations[13][14] of domestic violence and abuse against the other parent in order to retain control over their fears of abandonment and inferiority or to cover up their own abusive behavior and poor parenting.

Figuring out which of these fears makes your Crazy tick can help you better protect yourself and your family against her, which we will discuss in Part Three.

HCPs/Crazy love going to court. Love, love, *love* it. First, the court system is adversarial. There is a winner and a loser, and Crazy wants to win, which is just one of the reasons mediation is rarely effective in high-conflict divorce. Another is that Crazy views compromise as weakness. Second, going to court feeds her victim identity. Unless Crazy has acute social anxiety, going to court to recount how she has been harmed and to see her target punished produces a conflict buzz like nothing else.

HCPs/Crazy have poor problem-solving and conflict resolutions skills. This is another reason Crazy is a frequent flier in the legal system. The more problems she has, the more she blames her target(s). One can often identify this behavior by the disproportionate and extreme emotional intensity of Crazy toward her target.

HCPs and Crazy are also plagued by cognitive distortions and other forms of emotional reasoning[15] such as black and white thinking, jumping to conclusions, exaggerated fears and projection, much more so than non-HCPs. When Crazy is faced with contradictory information that threatens and confuses her emotional based reasoning and fragile self-image, she rigidly ignores the accurate information and vehemently defends her distortions, with high emotional intensity.

HCPs/Crazy have limited self-awareness. Due to the chaos and distress caused by her emotional reasoning, HCPs typically go from one emotional crisis to the next and one grievance to the next. HCPs and Crazy collect personal grievances like some kids collect baseball cards.

Most people take time to reflect upon their mistakes and successes in order to problem-solve and change for the better. Not so with HCPs or Crazy. HCPs put all of their emotions into attacking the target—trying to get them to change, to stop doing something, to compensate them for their troubles, or simply to divert attention from their own bad behavior.[16]

One of the defining characteristics of Crazy is that she doesn't believe she needs to change anything about herself. She expects everyone to unconditionally accept and love her. She places no such expectation on herself. Crazy refuses to change while insisting that others, reality and the world itself change to accommodate her.

Tying It All Together

The Fearsome Foursome—victim identity, entitlement, control freakery and emotional reasoning—are also at play in HCPs. Remember, this is how Crazy logic works:

> *I have been wronged. I am a victim. I am special. I am a special victim. I am owed. You must agree with me and do everything I want. You must think and feel exactly as I do. If you don't, you are abusing and trying to control me. I feel you are wrong, so you are. I don't care what really happened. I know what I feel. Facts are refutable. You are making me feel bad, so you must be bad. Because you are making me feel bad about myself by setting boundaries, not putting up with my bullying and unreasonable expectations and demands you must be punished. I am a victim and I demand justice.*

This is what drives high-conflict divorce and custody disputes, the custody games after the divorce is finalized and the frequent trips back to family court. Crazy wants to tattle on you for imagined transgressions, feel heard and get whatever it is she feels she is owed—usually someone else's hard earned money.

Takeaways

- Crazy thrives on conflict. It is her lifeblood. Never forget that and never assume anything else. She will always take the road of most conflict possible unless she has a strong motivation or self-interest not to do so.

- Crazy will never act in the best interest of the kids. Her hate and anger overshadow any love she has for them. It's part of why she's crazy. The only time she acts in the best interests of the children is if it lines up with her own selfish interests.

- The issue is not the issue. Nor is the issue your problem.

- HCPs and Crazy love court. Since they love it, accept that the only way to structure things with Crazy is via legal avenues.

- Crazy is never at fault. Ignore that. Stick to the facts and nothing more. HCPs are masters at baiting their targets. Just because she says something doesn't make it true. Just because she puts it in writing doesn't make it true either, regardless of what she chooses to believe.

Chapter 4

Personality Disorders: You Can't Argue with a Sick Mind

Dealing with a high-conflict, abusive ex-wife—Crazy—frequently means that you are also dealing with an individual who has what is known as a personality disorder (PD). What we see in this population of Crazy is primarily Borderline Personality Disorder (BPD), Histrionic Personality Disorder (HPD) or Narcissistic Personality Disorder (NPD).

There are other kinds of personality disorders, but we will focus on these three because one of these three disorders are most likely what you are dealing with. Making you an expert on personality disorders isn't in the least helpful. Always remember, the only thing we help Crazy with is finding the door. Hopefully, a better understanding of these disorders will give you some incentive to do that a little more quickly.

Before we get started, we need to address the internecine workings of the mental health field, specifically the APA (American Psychiatric Association). Politics, politics, politics!

The DSM (Diagnostic and Statistical Manual of Mental Disorders) is the "diagnostic bible" of mental health practitioners. It is currently on its fifth edition, which was released in 2013. In their ultimate wisdom, APA committee members decided to eliminate five of the ten personality disorders previously catalogued in the fourth edition of the DSM, including NPD and HPD.

Now, does this mean the narcissists and histrionics no longer exist?

Hope springs eternal, but no. They still exist and still cause problems for themselves and anyone who gets too close to them. So why did the APA do this?

Just because the APA removes a disorder from the DSM doesn't mean it magically disappears from the world. For example, Passive-Aggressive Personality Disorder is an actual characterological disorder people, mostly women, were diagnosed with as recently as the DSM-III. It was removed from the DSM-IV because women's groups felt it unfairly pathologized women (kind of like ADHD unfairly pathologizes boys, but we digress).

Chronically passive-aggressive individuals didn't automatically stop being passive-aggressive. The characterological symptoms were hidden under Personality Disorder Not Otherwise Specified due to political pressure.

Another example of the APA's vulnerability to political pressure can be seen in their refusal to include Parental Alienation Syndrome (PAS) and Hostile Aggressive Parenting (HAP) in the DSM. Numerous peer-reviewed studies have been done by credible researchers on PAS and HAP. If you have kids with Crazy, you know PAS is all too real. Nevertheless, it is not included in the DSM largely due to political pressure from NOW (the National Organization for Women) and similar feminist groups.

For the purposes of this discussion, we are going to pretend the DSM-V never happened, and use the definitions of BPD, HPD and NPD from the DSM-IV-R. If you are interested in more information about the APA and why they eliminated certain disorders from the most recent edition of its bible, there is an explanation of it on the Shrink4Men website.[12] We won't bore you with it here.

Borderline Personality Disorder

This is the personality disorder with the strangest name. The word *borderline* doesn't do anything to clue the average person in on what it means, so we are better off looking past the label and into the diagnostic criteria.

Here are the diagnostic items for BPD from the Diagnostic and Statistical Manual of Mental Disorders, 4th Edition, Revised (DSM-IV-R):

- Frantic efforts to avoid real or imagined abandonment. Note: Do not include suicidal or self-mutilating behavior covered in Criterion 5.

- A pattern of unstable and intense interpersonal relationships characterized by alternating between extremes of idealization and devaluation.

- Identity disturbance: markedly and persistently unstable self-image or sense of self.

- Impulsivity in at least two areas that are potentially self-damaging (e.g., spending, sex, substance abuse, reckless driving, binge eating). Note: Do not include suicidal or self-mutilating behavior covered in Criterion 5.

- Recurrent suicidal behavior, gestures, or threats, or self-mutilating behavior.

- Affective instability due to a marked reactivity of mood (e.g., intense episodic dysphoria, irritability, or anxiety usually lasting a few hours and only rarely more than a few days).

- Chronic feelings of emptiness.

- Inappropriate, intense anger or difficulty controlling anger (e.g., frequent displays of temper, constant anger, recurrent physical fights).

- Transient, stress-related paranoid ideation or severe dissociative symptoms.

The DSM-IV also adds the following:

The essential feature of Borderline Personality Disorder is a pervasive pattern of instability of interpersonal relationships, self-image, and affects, and marked impulsivity that begins by early adulthood and is present in a variety of contexts.

Histrionic Personality Disorder

This disorder's label also doesn't really give you a good idea of what you may be dealing with. Histrionics are often drama queens and attention whores. They display very intense emotions, however, the emotions are shallow. In other words, they typically engage in emotional theatrics for attention and not because they are actually in emotional distress.

The DSM-IV describes the disorder as a pervasive pattern of excessive emotionality and attention seeking, beginning by early adulthood and present in a variety of contexts, as indicated by five (or more) of the following:

- Is uncomfortable in situations in which he or she is not the center of attention.

- Interaction with others is often characterized by inappropriate sexually seductive or provocative behavior.

- Displays rapidly shifting and shallow expression of emotions.

- Consistently uses physical appearance to draw attention to self.

- Has a style of speech that is excessively impressionistic and lacking in detail.

- Shows self-dramatization, theatricality, and exaggerated expression of emotion.

- Is suggestible, i.e., easily influenced by others or circumstances.

Considers relationships to be more intimate than they actually are.

Narcissistic Personality Disorder

This disorder is one where the label is a good bit more explanatory to the average person. If you have heard of narcissism, or were ever married to it, then you already have a pretty good idea of what an NPD is and looking for the nearest exist when you encounter one.

The DSM-IV describes NPD as a pervasive pattern of grandiosity (in fantasy or behavior), need for admiration, and lack of empathy, beginning by early adulthood and present in a variety of contexts, as indicated by five (or more) of the following:

- Has a grandiose sense of self-importance (e.g., exaggerates achievements and talents, expects to be recognized as superior without commensurate achievements).

- Is preoccupied with fantasies of unlimited success, power, brilliance, beauty, or ideal love.

- Believes that he or she is "special" and unique and can only be understood by, or should associate with, other special or high-status people (or institutions)

- Requires excessive admiration.

- Has a sense of entitlement, i.e., unreasonable expectations of especially favorable treatment or automatic compliance with his or her expectations.

- Is interpersonally exploitative, i.e., takes advantage of others to achieve his or her own ends.

- Lacks empathy: is unwilling to recognize or identify with the feelings and needs of others.

- Is often envious of others or believes that others are envious of him or her.

- Shows arrogant, haughty behaviors or attitudes.

Any of this sound familiar? Any of this sound so familiar that you've wanted to pull your own hair out by the roots?

Now, there is a lot of other information we could give you about personality disorders and personality disorder traits. Then again, we made a promise from the outset of this book not to waste your time.

You see, while it may help you to have an understanding of what constitutes a personality disorder, it does absolutely nothing for you in terms of giving you a direction on what to do about it. In fact, it may do just the opposite for some people, pulling them further into the problem.

We have talked with many individuals who have become hung up on clinical terminology and diagnoses. Often, these people are still in the bargaining phase of their grief and are looking for magical remedies. They want to believe that if they could get the disordered person into the right treatment, or get them connected to a mental health professional who really knows what they are doing, or get them on the right kind of medicine then they would see improvement in the behaviors that have been so damaging to everyone involved.

This kind of belief, as it relates to people with a personality disorder, is a very misguided and unhealthy fantasy, and the sooner disposed with the sooner everyone involved can actually start to solve problems.

There is no FDA approved medication for personality disorders. The most that clinical professionals can hope to do with medicines is tranquilize the patient or treat their secondary problems, like depression or anxiety.

By the way, for those who are tenacious about getting them help, treating the depression does not in any way improve the personality disorder itself. If she was making you miserable before getting help with her depression, she will continue to make you miserable afterward. She will just feel a little better while doing it.

There is no kind of psychotherapy that is known to reliably improve people with personality disorders. None. Zero. Nada. *Capiche*?

Dialectical Behavior Therapy (DBT) was developed by Marsha Linehan, an individual with BPD, as a cognitive behavioral treatment for borderlines. It may provide some relief by improving impulse control, teaching the BPD individual the consequences for not considering other people's needs, feelings and rights and reality testing their emotions. However, only a small percentage of individuals with BPD are properly diagnosed and an even smaller percentage successfully progress through treatment. Please consider possible methodological weaknesses and/or ideological bias that may be present in research that touts DBT as a miracle cure for BPD.

Common weaknesses are too small sample size, questionable sample selection, e.g., all subjects were from upper middleclass Caucasian women. Also consider the background of researchers. We suggest you use Google to look into their background. Strong affiliations with gender studies programs, funding by BPD advocacy groups and in some cases the researchers themselves having BPD may be obvious reasons for skewed or overly optimistic results. The same holds true for practitioners who profit from providing recommended treatments.

Consider this in a different way. Most of us have heard the word sociopath. *Sociopath* is just another name for a person with Antisocial Personality Disorder. These individuals are marked by a lack of empathy, shallow emotions, remorselessness, and other antisocial behaviors. They can often be charming and socially adept in the short term, but can quickly turn criminal, sadistic and even murderous when it suits their purpose. They will feel absolutely nothing for the innocent people they harm.

Now, have you ever read or heard of a book about how to get along with a sociopath? How about a Cosmo article on "How to get that sociopath boyfriend to commit?" Do you ever hear people say, "Hey, we're trying to get help for our cousin, the sociopath?"

Of course not. Why? Because trying to find any kind of peaceful or even safe coexistence with a sociopath is incredibly stupid. Most people who know what a sociopath is choose not to be around them. We don't send them to a therapist who specializes in sociopaths (aside from the ones who work in prisons). We simply lock our doors, call the cops and do whatever else we need to do to make them go away. It's a matter of survival and common sense.

Choosing to ignore that by putting your focus on getting them help may make you feel good, but it does nothing more than feed their desire to control you. Inevitably, you will find yourself, once again, doing the work for Crazy that Crazy needs to do for herself. It also places you and the people close to you at continued risk.

Understand this: Borderlines, Histrionics and Narcissists are the sociopaths of relationship and family life. In fact, Antisocial Personality Disorder is grouped together with BPD, NPD and HPD, and together these 4 disorders comprise the Cluster B, or dramatic personality disorders. While they are typically not killers or criminals (unless you count false accusations, domestic violence and child abuse) these personalities are destructive harbingers of ill that will inflict all manner of damage without a shred of guilt to stop them.

In fact, they are actually worse than that. The typical reaction of a BPD/NPD/HPD to being caught in lies, manipulations and other destructive actions, is to attack whomever caught them, and portray themselves as victims who have been denied empathy and understanding. It is our opinion that BPDs, NPDs and HPDs are self-pitying sociopaths.

What the DSM-IV does not paint as explicitly as it could is that accountability for their actions is nonexistent in these individuals. They will slide a knife into your back and blame you for getting blood on the carpet. They will point to the red streak soaking your shirt and the crimson pool at your feet and say it's proof that you caused the stain. They will insist you made them do it.

After years of therapy and all the understanding and sympathy that can be extracted from people around them, they will do the exact same thing. Again, and again, and again. Remember, Crazy does not get better. Ever. Believing that Crazy will change is its own form of crazy.

Some people will argue that people with personality disorders are mentally ill and therefore not responsible for their behaviors and can't help the way they behave. This is ridiculous, especially if your Crazy can behave herself in court or in any other setting in which she wants to make a favorable impression.

Personality disordered individuals are not mentally ill in the same way that someone with schizophrenia or bipolar disorder are ill. Personality disorders are better described as *characterological disorders*. In other words, a person of poor character.

It's not that Crazy doesn't know right from wrong. She does. She just doesn't care if doing wrong gets her what she wants. Crazy is typically capable of recognizing when other people behave badly or criminally. The problem is she doesn't think the same codes of conduct, decency and law apply to her.

So, our final word on personality disorders is that you might as well understand what they are as you have a bird's eye view of what they do every day of your lives. The only reason the information is useful is that if you understand it correctly, it gives you even more reasons to say goodbye to Crazy.

Takeaways

- Personality disorders are best described as characterological disorders—a person of poor character.

- Don't get caught up in diagnosing Crazy or forcing her into therapeutic situations. Understand the diagnosis only to protect yourself, your children and your family.

- People with personality disorders are harmful to those around them. Please, let us repeat that: People with personality disorders are harmful to those around them. This includes your children, you and your spouse as you are forced to deal with them until the children are no longer minors.

- Being personality disordered is not an excuse to be a selfish, destructive asshole.

Chapter 5

The Golden Uterus

As discussed in Chapter 2, *What Makes Crazy Crazy: The Fearsome Foursome,* there are many varieties of Crazy. One of the most common and troubling forms of Crazy is the Golden Uterus. In addition to being a card-carrying member of the Sisterhood of Professional Victimhood, Crazy is also a member of the Golden Uterus Club, of which every member is more special than the next.

Golden Uterus is an admittedly snide, but completely accurate term for a mother who believes, that she is special and entitled simply by virtue of having given birth to or adopting a child.

A Golden Uterus is like a prima donna shrieking orders at everyone, from stagehands to the director of the show, not for any legitimate reason, but just to ensure that everyone knows who is really in charge. In more layman's terms, she is an obnoxious, insufferable bitch.

So what makes a mother a Golden Uterus?

Ownership. This kind of mother sees her children as possessions, rather than as their own persons. They only exist in relation to her. She derives a sense of absolute, unilateral power over the children and their father because she is the mother. She truly believes the children exclusively belong to her. She may rent them out to their fathers on occasion, but they are HER children.

That is, until the kids screw up or develop severe emotional problems. Then, in her communications with their father, they suddenly go from being MY children to YOUR children. It doesn't matter that the Golden Uterus has majority custody and has done the bulk of the parenting because she chose to relegate dad to role of wallet and babysitter. If the kids have problems it's not her fault. It's his fault.

Symbiosis. The Golden Uterus and her children are a "two-fer," meaning dad doesn't get to have his own relationship with the kids separate from her. This is especially evident during and after divorce. If dad wants to see the kids, she is part of the deal. It's common for the Golden Uterus to tell her ex, "The children feel . . ." or "The children want . . ." or "The children need . . ." In reality, the children don't feel, want or need—it is her feelings, her wants and her needs. She just projects them onto the children, and if her ex doesn't comply, he's a bad dad.

The Golden Uterus is the epitome of the adage, "If momma isn't happy, no one's happy." Regardless of her overinflated sense of worth, she is often a lousy, if not downright abusive parent. She frequently confuses her best interests with the best interests of the children. As you well know, mom's best interests and the children's best interest aren't always synonymous.

For example, it is not in the children's best interest for the Golden Uterus to block access to their father, nor is it in the children's best interest to bankrupt their father because she *chooses* not to work. It is also not in the children's best interests to be forced to choose between loving either mom or dad. The Golden Uterus views the children loving and wanting to have a healthy relationship with their father as an act of disloyalty.

Entitlement. The Golden Uterus believes her loins are hallowed ground; that the biological act of having a child makes her superior and entitles her to special privileges. Let's use her refusal to work or insistence on being underemployed post-divorce as an example again. Staying at home is a legitimate choice for either parent, if that's what the couple decides when they're together. After divorce, her refusal to work is her own choice and her own responsibility. It is what she has unilaterally decided to do because the courts will collect the money for her. She will claim, with a straight face, that it's in the children's best interest for her to stay home and post on Facebook and the Mom-o-sphere while the kids are in school rather than get a job and, heaven forbid, contribute to the children's care.

Just do some surfing on websites that cater to moms, Cafemom. com, for instance. There are forums dedicated to helping women navigate the legal tangle of family law. You will find women asking how to get the most support possible out of their children's father. Be it child support, alimony, orders to pay for medical issues or activity costs or how to ensure they, the moms, get as much state aid as possible. All the while insisting the father front any and all costs that can be attributed in some way to the child(ren).

Rarely is concern expressed regarding when dad should see his children or continue his relationship with them. In these forums, it's seen as completely acceptable that dad get the bare minimum required by the state regarding time with his kids, but he will pay for that time—it's his obligation.

Now we realize we are making generalizations, but where else do you see such blatant entitlement?

Eats her young. The Golden Uterus expects not only her ex to sacrifice everything to her, but the children as well. In many cases, her children *are* the sacrifice; to her financial needs, her desire for revenge, her desire for aggrandizement or to feel loved. There is often a role reversal in the parent-child relationship of the Golden Uterus in which she expects the kids to tend to her emotional needs rather than the other way around. This reversal is known as parentification.

The Golden Uterus often has poor or no boundaries with the kids. Children aren't allowed to have their own feelings and opinions. They're expected to be mirrors to the Golden Uterus. If mommy is sad, then child must be sad. If mommy is mad, then child must be mad. If mommy hates daddy and his new wife, then child must hate daddy and his new wife. These mothers wield guilt, fear and obligation over their children with staggering efficiency.

Even after the kids grow up, the Golden Uterus believes she should still come first and take precedence over her adult children's spouse and children. They owe her because she is their mother. In extreme cases, the Golden Uterus will sabotage her children's maturational development in order to keep them infantilized and dependent, so she can maintain her special "Mother" status for as long as possible.

Fathers are disposable. Dad is not permitted to have boundaries either. Boundaries are viewed as a challenge to her authority, a form of "abuse" or an attempt to control her. Fathers are a financial and emotional welfare system for the Golden Uterus, and she is forever on the dole. She doesn't want input regarding how the children are raised, even if joint decision-making is specified in a court order. The court does not tell the Golden Uterus what to do. Like everything and everyone else, the court is there for her to use however she sees fit.

Servitude is forever. The Golden Uterus is the gatekeeper of the children's relationship with their father and anyone else in his life, including you. She will impose herself into the children's relationship with their father and use her "Mother of the Children" status to disrupt your relationship with your husband, if she can. Should she recouple, however, it is none of your husband's damn business. She may even try to install her new victim as the shinier, newer, better daddy and banish your husband from the children's lives altogether.

Divorce does not signify the end of the marriage to the Golden Uterus. It just changes the environment in which she exerts her sick control. She believes her ex is still her property and owes her for life, no matter what the court documents say. He is expected to remain on alert, ready to mobilize whenever she wants something. Even if he remarries and has other children, the Golden Uterus still expects her needs to come first.

"I don't care if your other child needs to have ear surgery so she can hear. Your first child expects to go to arts and crafts camp. No, child support does NOT cover it. Child support is for me to decide how to spend. Me? Get a job? Why? So you and your new wife can live it up? Screw you, buddy. You made a promise to ME, and you're going to keep it."

Ultimately, the Golden Uterus wants complete control and power over others and zero accountability and zero responsibility, and no one knows this better than you. Anyone who has had to deal with a high-conflict ex-wife and mother knows all too well the phenomena described in this chapter.

Unfortunately, the Golden Uterus is greatly enabled and legitimized by both our mommy-worshipping culture, politicians, law enforcement and the family courts. The exalted, untouchable position of Bearer of the Golden Uterus, that divinely ordained reproductive organ makes her word and wishes akin to those of a living God. It would be much easier to neutralize the destructive impact of the Golden Uterus in your own life if this were not the case.

As the bearer, keeper and legal owner of the children, our society confers on the Golden Uterus an absolute and unquestioned assumption of wisdom, maturity, intelligence and the moral acumen to both act with integrity and instill good values in her offspring.

In fact, that is such a rigid social requirement that most people in our culture will fail to see the destructive acts of a dysfunctional mother even when they occur right in front of their eyes. After all, that is what a Golden Uterus is: a severely dysfunctional mother and emotionally underdeveloped, spoiled child in an adult body.

We see this all the time as custodial mothers alienate their children from their fathers, permanently scarring their minds out of a desire for personal revenge. We see this all the time as new wives and girlfriends are vilified, marginalized and, in extreme but not uncommon cases, harassed and stalked. Many people see this happening, but nobody can do anything about it. We have no social or legal mechanism in place to stop an alienating Golden Uterus mother bent on destruction.

This is how we sacrifice children to the Golden Uterus. We abandon them to participate in the deification of their abusers.

A mother playing games with visitation and support orders isn't just playing games, she is playing God. She is exerting the power to control the life's destiny of her child, distorting all their future relationships as well as their sense of self-worth. She often has the power to incarcerate the father, to bring additional financial distress, and she wields it with self-serving, adolescent enthusiasm.

When we elevate women to the level of deified Golden Uterus, we are constructing a sacrificial altar on which many children will suffer psychological trauma that may last a lifetime. We are also setting up a system of incredible financial abuse in which ex-husbands are forced to pay "tribute to pharaoh" just because they had the misfortune to choose a person of poor character as a wife.

Many men we have talked with have expressed repeated shock at the level of sadistic conduct that somehow became normalized *after* their divorce, including the ongoing psychological abuse of the children.

A Golden Uterus creates an environment where disrespect and condescension toward the father and his new partner is encouraged and openly practiced. Fathers who once had tight bonds with beloved children live to see those children openly parrot the disdain and contempt for him held by the mother. New stepmoms hoping to just be liked by their partners' children are disrespected and reviled.

The Golden Uterus phenomenon is just another facet of Crazy, but it is a particularly ugly and destructive one.

Takeaways

- The woman who sees herself as "The Mother," aka the Golden Uterus, is the gatekeeper to the children. She will fight vigorously and, if need be, viciously to keep that role.

-

- The Golden Uterus packages the children with her as a "two-fer"—you cannot have one without the other.

-

- Because of this, the kids are not allowed to be independent people. They are merely an extension of Crazy and what she wants.

-

- You may see your spouse and yourself as victims of parental alienation. Be prepared for this. It's one of the weapons in the arsenal of Crazy with a Golden Uterus complex.

-

- Parental alienation in all its ugly forms is really hard for the kids and targeted parents to overcome.

Chapter 6

Lie Down with Crazy, Wake Up with Fleas

Anyone who spends a significant amount of time with Crazy inevitably develops issues of his or her own. And, let's face it, anyone who has a pattern of being attracted to Crazy or stays with Crazy after the mask of sanity is removed, probably had issues long before Crazy came along.

Often, men and women who are attracted to Crazy have at least one parent who possesses similar characteristics. We learn about love from our parents, for better or worse. They teach us what is acceptable and unacceptable in our relationships. If you have a parent who made you her or his caregiver, confidante, peer, physical or emotional punching bag or surrogate spouse, you probably grew up basing a large part of your identity on being a codependent, fixer, rescuer, people-pleasing, eggshell tip-toeing, non-confrontational pushover—or you identified with the abusive parent and became Crazy. We assume that you are reading this book because you and your partner are the former and not the latter.

If you or your partner did not have abusive parent(s), but were raised to *always* be nice, to *always* turn the other cheek and to *always* do your best to get along with others, this also makes you a perfect target for Crazy. While these childhood teachings may have been well intentioned (and in a world free of Crazy, they very well might be), they are contributing to Crazy's ability to cut through you and your relationship like a hot knife through butter. In either case, you and your partner were groomed to be targets for Crazy. The behaviors and lessons you learned as a child that make you a target for Crazy are "fleas."

Fleas are maladaptive coping mechanisms developed in dysfunctional and abusive families and in dysfunctional and abusive adult relationships. We think it's high time for a flea dip.

Turning the other cheek in the face of Crazy's assaults will only leave you bruised, battered and punch drunk. Tiptoeing around Crazy enables her worst behaviors because you are adapting your life to Crazy. Appeasing Crazy does not work either. Giving into bullying and other noxious behaviors only reinforces Crazy by teaching her that if she escalates the lies, manipulations, intimidations and extortions, you will eventually concede to her demands.

While married to Crazy, your husband probably learned very quickly that if he did not do Crazy's bidding, there would be hell to pay. Rage outs, name-calling, guilt trips, the silent treatment, degrading him, undermining his role as father, telephone or text harassment at inopportune times (e.g., 60 text messages while at work), threats to call his boss, family or friends to vilify him, withholding affection and sex, etc., are the most common tactics in Crazy's bag of tricks. In a futile effort to keep the peace, your husband probably learned that it was easier in the short run to give in to Crazy. This flea will likely be one of your biggest obstacles in saying goodbye to Crazy.

If your husband was unable to set limits, enforce boundaries and stand up to Crazy during their marriage, it is no surprise that he is still unable to do so—especially if he has a conflict-avoidant or people-pleasing nature. If Crazy has hostages by way of shared children, it will be more difficult for your partner not to crumble in the face of Crazy's escalating tantrums and manipulations once he finally begins to enforce boundaries, detach and tell Crazy, "No."

What happens when a child throws a tantrum after being told no to her request for a cookie, and you give her the cookie to calm her down? The child learns that pitching a fit will get her what she wants.

What happens if you don't give the child a cookie right away at the onset of the next tantrum? The child pitches an even bigger fit until she gets what she wants. The same is true of Crazy. Unfortunately, you can't put Crazy in a timeout chair, but you *can* stop rewarding her problematic behaviors. Doing so will, hopefully, either extinguish them or reduce the intensity and frequency in order to insulate your family and minimize the impact of Crazy.

This is not as easy as it sounds. If you implement the techniques described in this book, things will probably get worse before they get better. You and your partner will need to present a united front as you ride out Crazy's extinction bursts.

What's an extinction burst?

An extinction burst is what occurred in the example of the tantrum throwing child and the cookie. Once a child's bad behavior has been rewarded, the child will persist in that behavior in order to obtain whatever it is she wants—a cookie, a toy, money, your attention, the keys to the car, a new iPhone, a new computer, etc. As a parent, you know you cannot keep rewarding the bad behavior. You must set limits and not give in to the tantrums, the pestering, the guilt trips, high-pressure tactics and other forms of acting out.

Typically, the child will not accept the new boundary right away. Instead, she will increase the bad behavior until you give in or until the child wears herself out and realizes the bad behavior will no longer work. Relent even once and reward the child (or Crazy) and you undo all your hard work because you have taught the child (or Crazy) that if she behaves like a bigger brat, she will get her way.

The extinction burst is the escalation of the bad behavior before it is extinguished. It is a behavioral psychology term. In writing this book, we decided to avoid using too many psychology terms, but extinction burst is a great term. It calls to mind the scene in *Jurassic Park* when the velociraptors are throwing themselves against the fence in a frenzy trying to find a weak link so they can enter the park and wreak havoc and destruction. Crazy is the velociraptor. You and your partner are the fence. Your fleas are the weak links.

Other common fleas you and your partner may be struggling with are a need to be seen as the good guy, a need for approval, a fear of loss, learned helplessness, early childhood conditioning to be a people pleaser, a fear of anger, conflict and confrontation, pervasive feelings of guilt and an exaggerated sense of obligation. There may be other fleas, but these are the most common in our experience.

Fleas are not terminal, but they can be damned hard to get rid of—hard, but not impossible. As you and your partner stand your ground, Crazy will up the ante. She may withhold visitation, lie to the children and anyone else who will listen, cry to her lawyer, file vexatious hearings so Daddy or Mommy Judge will set him straight. Yes, this probably sounds like the last thing you want—Crazy on steroids. Once you decide to say goodbye to Crazy, you cannot blink, no matter how much she ups the ante.

Takeaways

- The time spent with Crazy means issues for your partner and for you.

- You may also have issues due to past problems with one or both of your parents, or you may simply have issues with Crazy because you were raised to treat people with respect and kindness and to give them the benefit of the doubt.

- Any or all of the above can give you fleas—the coping mechanisms that allow us to deal with Crazy.

- When shaking off fleas, things with Crazy can get worse before they get better.

- It's not impossible to get rid of fleas, but it is hard. Stick with it.

Chapter 7

Parental Alienation Syndrome: Brainwashing and Weaponizing Children

If you have done even a tiny amount of research to try to understand what is wrong with Crazy, you have probably stumbled across the terms hostile aggressive parenting (HAP) and parental alienation syndrome (PAS). Much like divorce and bitterness, HAP and PAS are another dysfunctional duo. HAP can lead to PAS. In other words, hostile aggressive parenting behaviors are the actions and parental alienation is the consequence.

Both mother and fathers can be alienators, although a PAS campaign is much easier to conduct for custodial parent than it is for non-custodial parent. This is because the custodial parent has more access and thus more opportunity to cajole, manipulate, brainwash and intimidate children into hating and/or fearing the other parent. The most recent statistics from the U.S. Census Bureau indicate that women receive primary custody in 82% of custody cases, which means women have more opportunity to engage in hostile aggressive parenting.

Hate is a poison that can spread very quickly if unchecked. All an alienating parent needs to be successful is access. Irreparable damage can be done in as little as two weeks. If Crazy has the kids at least 50% of the time or more, that's all she needs to inflict significant damage.

Organizations like NOW (the National Organization for Women) and domestic violence groups deny that parental alienation is real. They claim PAS is a ploy by abusive men to steal children from their mothers. Of course, NOW does believe abuse by proxy is real, except that men are the perpetrators of it and only women can be the victims.

If you're dealing with Crazy, you know PAS is all too real. You have seen its destructive and heart-breaking effects firsthand. It has probably led to many uncomfortable moments and arguments about Crazy and the children, especially if the children are acting out and being disrespectful toward you and their father. When you combine PAS and Daddy Guilt, which we discuss in *chapter 17*, you have a potential minefield that has undoubtedly caused you to do a lot of tiptoeing around that damned elephant and its calves parked in your living room.

What Is Parental Alienation?

In the simplest terms, parental alienation is the programming and brainwashing of children to hate and/or fear the other or "target" parent.[18] When the target parent recouples, alienation efforts can also be aimed at the new partner as well. Parental alienation is a form of child abuse. It is also abuse toward the targeted parent by the alienating parent.

Parental alienation is a form of splitting, or seeing people as either all good or all bad, and mobbing, which is group victimization of a single target. One frequently sees this behavior among child and adult bullies. For example, when a "mean girl" becomes angry with a friend, she enlists their peer group to also be angry with and exclude the targeted child from peer relations. The goal is to humiliate, demean, discredit, and isolate the target.

The mindset is: *"Because I'm mad at Meaghan, I want everyone else to hate and be mad at Meaghan, too. If you don't hate Meaghan like I do, then you're not my friend either."* Switch "Meaghan" to "your father" and it is essentially the same phenomenon—except that teaching and/or insisting a child hate the other parent is teaching children to hate half of themselves. Crazy puts the kids in a loyalty bind—Crazy vs. daddy. Crazy essentially forces the kids to choose between her or their dad.

By now it should come as no surprise that most cases of parental alienation occur in relationships that have a high degree of conflict, abuse, mental illness and/or personality disorders such as BPD, NPD, HPD and PPD (Paranoid Personality Disorder) and high anxiety parents. It is often also part of the scorched-earth policy Crazy wages upon her ex. If Crazy can successfully alienate the children from your husband and you, she "wins." In this respect, Crazy turns children into weapons and war trophies.

Crazy basically programs the kids to view everything you say and do—no matter how neutral—negatively. For example, your husband is uncharacteristically 15 minutes late for the scheduled custody pick-up. Crazy tells the kids, *"A good parent who really loves his kids would be on time,"* which means, *"Your father is a bad parent who doesn't love you."* It is a negative interpretation of a neutral event. Crazy doesn't allow for neutral interpretations like heavy traffic, a flat tire or being held up at work. She seizes every opportunity to "prove" her targets are bad people who don't love them.

These messages can be explicit or implicit, conscious or unconscious, and include verbal and non-verbal cues and rewards, as well as punishment for the children.[19] For example, Crazy wants the kids to hate her targets and be as angry with them as she is. So what does she do?

She makes faces and rolls her eyes when the kids talk about their father or you. She tries to instill fear in the children toward their father and you by trying to portray the two of you as incompetent, uncaring and, possibly, dangerous. For example, after the kids return from visitation, she says things like, "Did he remember to feed you? Are you scared sleeping there at night? Do they drink a lot of wine with dinner? If he ever touches you or says anything to make you uncomfortable, just call me and I'll call the police. You can come home if you want to—just call me, and I'll come and get you. You have more fun with me, don't you? If it weren't for me making your father take care of us, he'd spend all his money on his new wife and her kids, and we wouldn't have a roof over our heads. I'm so lonely when you're with your father. I cry the entire time you're gone."

Crazy may also enlist negative advocates (enablers) such as friends, family, church members, therapists and the court system to help her successfully alienate. The most difficult cases of alienation are the ones in which the children are enthusiastic accomplices in their own victimization and the victimization of the targeted parent.

Children Who Are Willing Participants in Parental Alienation

Your stepchildren probably learned some powerful lessons about relationships by watching their father be abused and undermined by Crazy, especially if they had a "no talk" policy about the rages, flimsy or non-existent boundaries, yelling, emotional withdrawal, cold silences, name-calling and other forms of disparagement. Children are adversely affected by witnessing constant conflict and abuse, no matter their age.

Oftentimes, alienated parents don't understand why the children seem to be siding with Crazy—especially if he did most of the caretaking and nurturing. There are several reasons the kids choose Crazy and participate in their own alienation.

Fear. Crazy is scary when on the attack, which probably makes it all the more confusing to see the children against your husband. Why wouldn't they turn against her when she is so mean and angry? Children depend upon their custodial parent. Seeing Crazy lose it and rage out of control or, conversely, playing the fragile victim, is anxiety provoking, if not downright terrifying to kids.

They saw how Crazy treated and treats their father and fear the same. They go along with the program of hate to keep Crazy's "love" and to avoid her wrath. It's like making friends with the school bully so she doesn't pick on you. We know of cases in which Crazy cut the kids' father out of old family photos, the way Joseph Stalin cut former political comrades out of photos once he deemed them to be "enemies of the people." The message is, "Anger me and you will cease to exist." In fact, this is one of the reasons many men stay with Crazy for as long as they do—fear of Crazy.

Anger. The kids are mad at their dad. He got out, they didn't. Maybe they're angry he isn't there anymore to intervene, act as a buffer, protect them or take the brunt of Crazy's crazy. Sometimes kids experience dad leaving as betrayal or abandonment—particularly when Crazy tells them it is. Even if they understand their parents didn't have a happy marriage, they still want mom and dad to be together. Possibly, your husband cheated on Crazy, and Crazy told the kids about it. In this case, the children may have some legitimate anger toward their father.

Psychological defense. The kids may participate in their alienation to defend against feeling loss or sadness. Children are not psychologically equipped to go through the grieving process any more than Crazy is. Of course, they can be guided through it, but not with Crazy at the helm. Pending other developmental milestones, kids typically do not have the psychological capacity to successfully navigate major loss until mid-adolescence. If Dad had died, the kids could idealize his memory.

Mourning the loss of someone not dead requires a level of psychological sophistication most children do not possess. Children need parents to help them navigate such a loss or change in circumstances. Instead, alienated children follow the alienating parent's script and vilify the physically absent parent because feeling angry is less anxiety provoking than sadness and grief.

Material gain. Crazy will often reward the kids with material goods, praise, affection, trips and fun activities in exchange for being cruel and disrespectful to Dad or refusing to see him. Kids who don't buy into Mom's vilification of Dad and the new wife are told they are bad and disloyal, lose privileges or have affection withheld from them.

In some cases, Crazy will become the "fun parent," meaning there are few rules and responsibilities at her house. She allows the kids to play video games for as long as they want, come and go as they please, allow boyfriends and girlfriends to sleep over, provide a steady diet of junk food, very few chores, etc. Then the kids go to dad's home where they're expected to do their homework, do age-appropriate chores and behave themselves. When consequences are enforced for misbehavior, the kids call Crazy to come get them.

Caretaking Crazy. The kids feel responsible to emotionally, and sometimes physically, take care of Crazy. They see how upset and out of control Crazy is and want to make her "better" or they're afraid she'll be sad if they spend time with their dad. When a child takes on the emotional or physical caretaking of a parent, they are parentified.

Parentification forces a child to shoulder emotions and responsibilities for which she or he isn't developmentally prepared. It is another form of child abuse and frequently occurs in alienation cases. Crazy dumps her emotional needs on the child who then becomes her confidante, champion, hero and/or surrogate spouse. This is extremely unhealthy as it robs children of their childhood and leads to difficulty in having normal adult relationships later in life.

Power. The kids see the power Crazy wields by behaving in an abusive and hurtful way toward their dad and realize they can wield the same power by acting out and hurting dad, too. A child or teenager's first taste of power can be thrilling for them. Of course, what they're learning from Crazy is how to gain control by being an emotionally abusive bully.

Attention. The more Crazy plays the professional victim to friends, family and the legal system, the more benefits she may gain— deferential treatment, sympathy, power, money and other assets. The kids mirror Crazy's victim mentality and behaviors and use it to net their own gains.

If the children your husband shares with Crazy have been alienated, it is probably due to some combination of these reasons. Even though most children are not consciously aware of what's occurring, it is generally a mistake to tolerate or ignore these behaviors. If you can get them into counseling with a qualified and competent therapist, we strongly encourage you to do so.

Takeaways

- This is a hard chapter. Parental alienation is very painful. Seeing the damage Crazy plays out with the kids is difficult to see and accept.

- Parental alienation is real.

- An aggressive alienator (which Crazy is) can spin anything into a way to negate and denigrate you and your spouse.

- Your spouse did not abandon the kids, no matter what Crazy says. Your spouse/partner left a marriage to Crazy.

- Kids do not have the ability to deal with the complexity of the emotions of grief and loss alone. They need a parent to help them. Crazy will never offer that to them.

- Everyone involved, other than Crazy, can be afraid to set boundaries as everyone has seen what Crazy will do. Fear of what Crazy will do is a powerful consequence for your spouse and the kids.

- Parental alienation is one more method of control for Crazy.

Chapter 8

Pointing a Crooked Finger: How Crazy Uses the Power of Lies to Abuse and Control Victims

---

March 2006. Crystal Gail Mangum, a stripper and "escort" falsely accused three male Duke University students of raping her. She came close to ruining their lives, and indeed those young men still live with the aftereffects of the allegations. Mangum was not prosecuted for the false report but was instead referred for counseling. She later murdered her boyfriend.

August 2009. Danmell Ndonye accused four young men of gang raping her in a Hofstra University men's dormitory restroom. The men were arrested and jailed. After three days of being incarcerated, a video surfaced showing that the sex had been consensual. Ndonye faced no criminal charges for her actions.

In May 2011 a maid, Nafissatou Diallo falsely accused Dominique Strauss-Kahn, the head of the International Monetary Fund and French presidential hopeful, of raping her in a New York hotel room. The accusation alone destroyed Strauss-Kahn's career, forcing him to resign his position as the head of the IMF and to forego any future political ambitions. Diallo was not prosecuted.

Those are three cases of false accusations that made national headlines. If you do any research into this subject, or if you happen to have a Crazy in your life, you know there are many more, that most of them never get attention from the media, and that those making the accusations are rarely punished for their actions.

Part of the difficulty in addressing the false allegation issue is the sheer scope of the problem. In June 2010 the Orlando, Florida police department issued a public statement, saying that false reporting has reached an epidemic level. They made a public plea to the community to stop the false reporting of rape because there were so many false reports that it was putting a stress on police resources and causing credibility problems for real rape victims. This happened even as the Orlando prosecutor's office shied away from going after false accusers.

That is just false criminal accusations of sexual assault, which actually represents only a fraction of the false allegation problem. Much more common is the occurrence of false allegations in family courts. In the United States alone there are more than one million restraining orders issued by family courts each year based on allegations that are either trivial or patently false. These orders, known as ex parte orders, require no evidence or corroboration and are routinely used as a part of divorce strategy in order to get the upper hand. They cause immeasurable damage to the individuals targeted.

Mark Mahnkey, Director of Public Policy and Media Relations for the Washington Civil Rights Council, called these orders the "biggest rollback of civil rights since the Jim Crow era."

Ex parte restraining orders are particularly attractive to Crazy. They allow her to alienate him from their children, remove him from the family home and put his life in a state of chaos from which it will be much harder to fight back in the divorce. It's harder to develop plans to defend yourself immediately after a sudden eviction, and this is often what happens to those men on the receiving end of these unfair orders.

If Crazy was gasoline, ex parte restraining orders are a lit match. Crazy loves them because they are a multipurpose tool of personal terrorism. With one she can demonize her partner, cripple him emotionally and financially, and make him look like the bad guy while she does it. It's Crazy's wet dream and winning lotto ticket all rolled up into one.

Again, so far we are only talking about false allegations in the legal sense. Crazy does not need a judge or a law enforcement officer to make a false allegation, and she often—even routinely—proves it.

As you go back through the path of Crazy's life, you often find it marked by one sort of false allegation after another. She will tell you that whatever wrongs she has committed in the past, whether they were affairs or some other form of abuse, were because others had allegedly wronged her first. It's the "he made me" defense, and she justifies it with a false allegation to make her appear to have acted in self-defense, rather than with the premeditation and malice that actually drive her actions.

If there are children involved, she has already told them a long list of things about their dad that are either not true or stretched beyond credibility. She has lied to friends and family at every turn: about him, about you, and about anyone who she imagines is not on her side.

A perfect example of this is when Crazy complains about child support. Crazy will tell everyone, the children included, that "your father" just "stopped" paying support, and anything lacking in their lives is due solely to "your father." The fact that your spouse/partner has paid, and continues to pay via the state's child support enforcement agency is irrelevant. There is a legal trail of documentation, but that doesn't matter to Crazy. Most people cannot or will not check into Crazy's lies.

She lies to turn people against her enemies and against each other, to elicit sympathy as a victim, to recruit others to fight for her cause, to create chaos and to exert whatever control she can on those around her.

She also does it out of sheer meanness, simply because she is a vindictive and unprincipled person, simply because she can.

Crazy relies on the fact that most people are decent and will not challenge her. Not even legally. Most people are not Crazy, and most people tell the truth. Crazy utilizes that assumption to further her goals.

It is this last explanation that is perhaps most helpful to those who have decided to say goodbye to Crazy. In the end, Crazy's motives for making a false accusation are not particularly relevant. It doesn't really matter if she lied to gain an upper hand in a divorce, or because she wanted to ruin the image of a father in the eyes of his children, or if she wants to get family members or others to take her side in a dispute. When all is said and done, Crazy is a dangerous liar, and she won't quit because the divorce was settled in her favor, or because children no longer trust their father or because the in-laws think she is a victim and take her side.

Whatever the outcome, Crazy will continue to lie, continue to falsely accuse, and as time goes by the accusations will become more severe.

If she was willing to lie to a judge to say her husband physically abused her and the children, and she is successful in getting away with it, she can and will allege even worse things, such as sexual abuse of children, if it fits her needs in the future, or if she just wants to inflict more damage.

So once again we find that seeking to understand her motives for this or any other of her destructive behaviors is a complete waste of time. You are much better off knowing what to do about it and how to protect yourself from it happening repeatedly down the road.

As we will repeat again and again through this book, less exposure is less vulnerability. The less of your life she is involved with, the less of your life she can attack.

Takeaways

- Crazy lies. About anything. Or everything. Whatever is convenient to her.

- Accept that Crazy can and will lie about everything.

- If her lies are accepted in court, she will escalate the scope of what she lies about.

- Crazy will always take advantage of the fact that others do not challenge her lies. One of the hallmarks of Crazy is using the decency of others to do what she wants.

- You cannot stop her lying.

- You must not try to stop the lying. Instead, accept that Crazy will lie and protect yourself and your family.

Chapter 9

Compassion for Crazy: or, Sympathy for the Devil

Does Crazy have problems? Undoubtedly. Does Crazy suffer from some kind of personality disorder or other mental health issue? Most likely. Did Crazy grow up in an incredibly dysfunctional and abusive family? Maybe, maybe not. Aren't we supposed to have compassion for people who have problems and/or who have mental health issues? In theory, yes, we should.

The problem with having compassion for Crazy is that Crazy will typically twist any sympathy, empathy or other human kindness you show her into a weapon to use against you. Ever hear the expression, "No good deed goes unpunished?" It was probably coined by someone burned by Crazy.

Being an angry, resentful, hate-filled, permanent victim and/or perpetually selfish child must be a miserable existence on many levels. In many cases, this kind of person only feels "happy" when she is hurting you, destroying someone or something you love or taking something from you. That is what Crazy calls "winning." In theory, it's okay to pity and have compassion for such a person. In reality, feeling sympathy for Crazy when you are still dealing with her week in and week out is a mistake.

Feeling sorry for Crazy is a slippery slope. Pity may make it more difficult to maintain effective boundaries, which is the fundamental key to coping with and neutralizing Crazy. Too many people allow sympathy to cloud their judgment and then fall into the trap of making excuses for and enabling Crazy. You may think (or be shamed into believing) that feeling sympathy for her makes you the better person. In reality, what it usually does is leave you vulnerable to more manipulation and attacks.

You cannot afford to have compassion for Crazy until you can do so *from a safe distance*. In other words, when you reach a point where Crazy can no longer harm you and your loved ones, then you can feel all sorts of sympathy for Crazy. Until such a time, you must protect yourself, and that means having a zero tolerance policy on Crazy.

Please do not confuse being cautious with your compassion for Crazy with being deliberately cruel to or openly contemptuous. When it comes to maliciousness, dirty tricks, manipulations, gaming the system, dishonesty, and distortions, Crazy has the home court advantage. Do not—we repeat—do not attempt to out-crazy Crazy or beat her at her game. All this does is bring you down to her level, and that is not a place we recommend calling home.

When you stoop to Crazy's level, Crazy wins. Most of Crazy's antics are consciously and unconsciously designed to elicit a reaction from her targets. If you react negatively, Crazy will more than likely flip the situation and portray you and your husband as the villains and herself as the victim. Do not give Crazy that kind of ammunition.

This book is going to drum a few basic ideas in your head over and over again. Setting and enforcing boundaries with Crazy and disengaging with Crazy to the greatest extent possible are the most effective strategies in minimizing and, hopefully, eradicating the effects of Crazy in your lives.

So, unless and until you and your husband can effectively maintain strong boundaries with the ex and not be tempted to take the bait when Crazy is intent on getting a rise out of you, it's probably best to save your compassion for yourselves.

Takeaways

- Compassion for Crazy will get you nowhere. She's got issues, but that is not an excuse for her behavior.

- Crazy will never reciprocate any compassion you may have for her.

- Compassion is only appropriate when you are at a safe distance from Crazy.

- Do not allow compassion to weaken your boundaries in regards to Crazy. She is not a friend to your family.

- Don't try to out-crazy Crazy. You will not win.

Chapter 10

The Dangers of Labeling Crazy "Crazy"

Many authors and experts in this field will caution you not to use labels regarding Crazy. This is unrealistic. "Ex-wife" is a label. "Stepmom" is a label. Human beings use labels and diagnoses as a mental shorthand to understand the world we live in and simplify our lives.

Some psychologists and other mental health professionals will tell you not to use diagnostic labels because you do not have the education and training to make such judgments. If you have a reasonable amount of intelligence, have read the DSM criteria for the group of personality disorders from which Crazy is known to typically suffer, and it matches your experience of Crazy as observed over time, odds are there is probably some validity to your layperson's diagnosis.

Some mental health professionals will tell you not to use diagnostic labels because some people use them as weapons and a form of name-calling. These same professionals also deliberately avoid making diagnoses of personality disorders for a number of reasons— namely liability, insurance won't pay for it and/or they don't want to lose a client.

Crazy may also evade formal diagnosis because she can be quite skilled at fooling therapists. As you know, she is adept at portraying herself as a misunderstood, long-suffering victim. Furthermore, the field of Psychology and Social Work is incredibly female-biased in that mental health professionals are trained to view women as victims and men as emotionally constipated, potential abusers. Therefore, the fact that Crazy may have worked with a therapist and not received a diagnosis may not mean anything other than:

- Crazy was able to pull the wool over the therapist's eyes.

- The therapist has not made a proper diagnosis because of insurance reasons, such as the therapist wants to be paid.

- The therapist does not want Crazy to terminate treatment because the therapist wants to be paid. When a therapist tells Crazy the truth and holds her accountable, Crazy usually bolts from therapy.

- The therapist is Crazy, too, and identifies with her or his patient.

- The therapist is so biased and indoctrinated in the "women as victims" dogma as to be blind to the fact that Crazy is, in fact, crazy.

- The therapist is afraid of being sued if they give Crazy a personality disorder diagnosis.

Why You Really Shouldn't Label Crazy "Crazy"

Crazy can and will turn any hint of being labelled around on you if given the opportunity. It is common for people who are forced to deal with Crazy to have the magical and often misguided belief that telling Crazy you believe she suffers from a personality disorder will cause her to have an epiphany, see the error of her ways and get help. So, should you tell Crazy she is crazy?

The answer is a resounding, "No." There are so many ways for that to go sideways!

Remember, this book is for YOU. Not Crazy. Crazy can't accept the reality of the divorce. Why would Crazy accept that she is, in fact, crazy? No need to waste resources on something that will not help you in any fashion.

Crazy will not accept your ideas or your help, and you will be on the receiving end of the attack to end all attacks. She'll come at you with all guns blazing. Resist the urge to try to help Crazy help herself. She doesn't want help. She wants to continue to be *enabled*—BIG difference. She's fine with the way she is, even if she's Crazy because she's miserable.

Fixing Crazy is neither your concern nor your problem. Telling her she's crazy and encouraging her to seek help is wanting to fix her. You can't.

So don't. Don't waste your time in engaging your efforts in a battle you will not win. YOU know she's crazy. That's what matters—the knowledge you have and how you use it to put up boundaries that allow you to have a peaceful life.

Takeaways

- Keep the idea that Crazy is crazy to yourself. Think of it as your secret weapon.

- Don't worry about forcing Crazy to be professionally diagnosed (unless it's legally ordered by the courts). If you do, she'll use that against you in every way she can.

- Use the knowledge of how Crazy is crazy to better fortify your boundaries. That's the very best use of this information.

Chapter 11

Gurus, Enablers, and Apologists

If you have had your life disrupted by a high-conflict, troublesome ex-wife or girlfriend, you are likely also no stranger to seeking help. After all, you are not reading this book by accident. We also assume that if you are like most people in your situation, this book is not your first attempt to find help. You have looked for help in one form or fashion before, possibly many times, and discovered there is little help available.

For what it is worth, this isn't your fault. The fact is that looking for practical answers from mental health professionals or the so-called self-help industry is an almost complete dead end. In fact, the entire mental health establishment, self-help gurus included, is much more likely to benefit Crazy than help you with your problems. Often, these professionals will only help Crazy do more damage than she was already doing.

This is true for a couple of reasons. One, Crazy is an expert at manipulation. She can expertly maneuver her way through systems, like family courts, and the officials that inhabit them. She can play the children against you, and even against their own father, quite easily. By playing the victim, she surreptitiously enlists the support of friends and other family members, even when she is clearly in the wrong.

We have to hand it to her; no one can play the puppeteer, even with mental health professionals, like Crazy. Even if the Crazy you deal with is not the sharpest tool in the shed, they are all masters at manipulation.

This brings us to the other problem. As discussed in the previous chapter, one of the things that makes it so easy for Crazy to get the upper hand with mental health professionals is that, just like the family courts, there is a pervasive bias in the mental health industry toward treating her like a victim no matter the evidence to the contrary. Rather than react appropriately to the destruction she is inflicting on you and others in your family and help you figure out a way to stop it, they will actually make things worse.

The average mental health practitioner is much more likely to encourage you to be patient with her and tolerate her intolerable behavior, than to help you take a stand against it—or to even acknowledge what you are going through in any meaningful way.

Understanding how and why this happens can be a very difficult pill to swallow, especially for women. Then again, we have promised you from the beginning of this book that we will be more concerned with reality than sparing anyone's feelings. We certainly had this chapter in mind when we told you that.

Crazy gets a pass from mental health professionals largely for the same reason she gets a pass from the courts and many other people. It is, first and foremost, because she is a woman. And yes, we know, you are likely a woman, too. But you are in this mess with a man by your side. Her position as a woman standing alone, especially if she has children, is a trump card in an industry that is geared to place women ahead of men.

It begins with feminist ideological influence on an industry where women are already the primary consumers, and it has been going on a long time.

This bias is most evident in the junk psychology market. Since the mid-eighties, get-rich-quick psychology gurus have made their way onto bestseller lists. It started with books like Robin Norwood's *Women Who Love Too Much*, the first blockbuster in a market that would become as reliable and permanent as rock-and-roll is to the music industry. As the title subtly implies, Norwood catered to women who saw themselves as faultless dupes in problematic relationships; women whose only fault was offering too much love to the wrong man. The subtext, of course, was that pretty much all men were the wrong man.

DR. TARA PALMATIER, PSYD & PAUL ELAM

Now, are there women who love too much? Sure. Is Crazy one of them? Hardly, but she gets the benefit of making the claim anyway.

Norwood's book was a man bashing runaway hit. It did not take long for the trend to follow the money—and to become more blatantly lopsided against men.

Susan Forward's *Men Who Hate Women and the Women Who Love Them* was next in line to top the bestseller list, and it was followed by many other highly successful books, all predicated on rigid stereotypes of men who hate and women who love. Men who are bad and women who are good.

It spawned a multi-billion dollar industry.

It has lasted to this day. Not long ago, Karen Salmansohn appeared on Fox News in a discussion on women executives. She was given a nice plug for her book, *Bounce Back*. They could have also given her credit for her previous publication, another bestseller, *How to Make Your Man Behave in 21 Days or Less Using the Secrets of Professional Dog Trainers.*

There is, perhaps, some tongue-in-cheek at play in that title, but it is still reflective of an industry, one that has helped shape the cultural consciousness about the relationships of men and women, that is geared to trivialize the problems men can and do face at the hands of women.

Why? Because that's where the money is, sadly enough. Our self-help industry has grown fat and lazy on the idea that women are victims and men are, well, just wrong. That worldview helps no one, but it sells.

Do you think that works pretty well for Crazy? Isn't that exactly what she pitches to anyone who will listen?

It isn't just book hawkers that are the problem.

The entire mental health industry is highly charged with sexual politics with anti-male feminist dogma guiding practitioners toward a paradigm that mimics exactly the worldview asserted in the self-help literature we have just addressed. The industry is populated with true believers in the idea that all women's problems are rooted in their victimization by men. It is a political ploy that just happens to have a deleterious effect on mental health.

In the real world, mental health depends greatly on a person's ability to be accountable for their own problems and solutions. Unfortunately, that is significantly less profitable than enabling people to view themselves as perpetual victims.

Here's the rub—and we are assuming you really don't need anyone to tell you this—all troubled relationships involve some amount of shared responsibility. Your partner can most likely look back on his relationship with Crazy and identify some things that were, in retrospect, mistakes. Most mental health professionals will give him a good pat on the back for saying so.

But when it comes to openly discussing the chaos, manipulations, sabotages, alienation, abuse and deceit that Crazy is committing and denying, those same mental health professionals will suddenly change gears and put it on you and him to handle this stuff rather than have her put a stop to her behaviors. Many of them will actually lead you to enable Crazy, even though she is not with you in the sessions.

Worse, many will do this even as children are being alienated and damage that cannot be undone is happening to your family. They simply have not been trained to help you confront and eliminate the abuses of a high-conflict, emotionally unbalanced female. They are more likely to be trained to put that burden on your male partner, despite it being clearly and obviously unmanageable.

You have now reached the point in this book where things are about to get a lot more interesting, productive and difficult.

We have hopefully identified the problem for you, and shed some light on some of the many obstacles to getting a grip on things and moving them in the right direction.

As you enter the pages ahead we are going to start talking about solutions—the things you can, indeed must do, if you want to find anything like freedom from this horrendously negative influence.

We are going to show you how this book is different from the ones we have just criticized, and why the suggestions we are going to make are vastly different from anything that has likely been suggested to you in the past.

It is not going to be easy.

If you think about it though, how easy are things now? How much fun are you having dealing with this individual who sometimes appears to be more monster than human?

We are going to test your resolve. And then test it again a few more times. We wish there was not a need for it, but we are not dealing in wishes, and we know that doing so would not help you.

There is some risk, too, to be fair and open. There is always a risk when dealing with Crazy. That fact alone has probably had you tolerating things that you never dreamed you would.

We assume, though, that you are here trying to figure out how to get your life back. That is precisely what we intend to help you do.

Takeaways

- The mental health industry has moved from responsibility for all to shifting blame in relationship issues to men. It's been immensely profitable.

- The mental health industry is unwilling to call Crazy crazy, for many reasons.

- Crazy is good at manipulating everyone, even mental health professionals.

- Realize that mental health professionals are not necessarily going to be allies in this battle. While disturbing, knowing it now allows you to move forward with open eyes.

Part Two

Preparing to Solve the Problem

As Part One demonstrated, there's a lot more to Crazy than, "His ex is still mad about the divorce." Crazy is only part of the problem, not all of the problem. A good many of the challenges that lie ahead in your efforts to say goodbye to Crazy are rooted in both you and your partner.

That's a hard thing to read, we know. Hard, but most likely the truth.

After all, it's Crazy who makes things difficult. It's Crazy who can't follow a court order to save her life. It's Crazy who tells the children everything about her custody "concerns," often with embellishment, if not outright lies. It's Crazy who trash talks your partner, you or anyone associated with you who has displeased her.

So why, you ask, are YOU among the obstacles?

Crazy has many weapons at her disposal. She counts on your reactions to them in order to succeed. Just eliciting an emotional response from you is a win for Crazy. This is especially true if Crazy can succeed in getting you to act out of anger or fear. She knows you are more prone to make mistakes when you are in emotional turmoil; mistakes that she will gladly use against you as soon as you make them.

We already know that self-improvement is not in Crazy's wheelhouse. We already know she cannot and will not stop the emotional taunting and manipulation. The only person you can do that for is you. The only way this situation will improve is if you and your partner make changes to how you respond and react to Crazy. If anything, she will try like crazy to sabotage you using the same old tools in her toolbox. We recommend that you not let her.

As you read Part Two, pay attention to your reactions. You may feel angry or defensive. That's okay. You're entitled to. Even so, that doesn't change the facts. In order for things to get better, you and your spouse must be the ones who make changes.

Recognizing what gets in the way of making changes is important. Being angry that you have to make changes is okay, too. It's perfectly normal and healthy to be angry that one crazy individual can cause so much havoc and dysfunction and harm in so many people's lives, getting away with it time and again, and that you are the one saddled with fixing the problem.

The good news is that you don't have to allow that anymore. Just because Crazy wants to make you feel angry and afraid doesn't mean that's how you have to feel. It is hard, and at times it may feel near impossible, but you can learn to prevent Crazy from getting under your skin.

This will require you to change how you manage your emotions and how you respond to Crazy. You will learn how to change your thinking and the rules of engagement with Crazy. In the process, you will grow and become stronger, and Crazy's ability to cause upset, chaos and misery will wither away.

Chapter 12

Are You Ready to Change?

Change, even desired change, can be extremely difficult to achieve. Several highly lucrative industries are built upon this truth. Consider the diet and nutrition industry, raking in billions of dollars annually with little or no impact on the health of the general population. Diets tend to fail because behavior is hard to change.

Sure, some very motivated self-starters do what they need to do long before they experience problems. However, many people don't really begin the process of change until or unless they begin to suffer severe consequences or the threat of severe consequences for not doing so.

Change—no matter how big or small, whether you're conscious of it or not—occurs in a series of stages. Two psychologists, James Prochaska and Carlo DiClemente, documented those stages.[20] How long you stay in each respective stage is variable and largely depends on you. Additionally, you may be in one stage, i.e., ready and eager to change, while your partner is stuck in an earlier stage. Obviously, this can present certain problems that we'll address in the next chapter.

For now, let's look at the stages of change described by Prochaska and DiClemente:

- **Precontemplation.** This stage can best be described as the "not ready to change" stage. Perhaps one of you does not see Crazy as a serious problem yet. Perhaps you or your husband view Crazy as a serious problem, but do not believe anything can be done about it. Perhaps you or your husband are afraid to take the steps necessary to say goodbye to Crazy because you are afraid of what she will do to retaliate. Maybe your husband feels discouraged and defeated before you even get started because his efforts to fix or help or reason with Crazy in the past have not worked. Now that you know fixing, helping or reasoning with Crazy is not possible, no wonder it didn't work!

Sometimes, when we're afraid to do something that will change our lives for the better—because we fear failure or another painful consequence—we avoid talking about it or even thinking about it. As you have already figured out, sticking your head in the sand for all things Crazy does not solve the problem. It just makes your butts better targets.

If any of this rings true for you or your husband, please consider another perspective. It's not that saying goodbye to Crazy is impossible. You were just approaching it the wrong way. Therefore, it may very well be worth the effort to try again, the right way.

- **Contemplation.** This is the "getting ready to change" stage. You're not quite ready to take action, but you're thinking about it, talking about it and figuring out what actions you will take when you are ready. For example, you and your husband agree you no longer want to live in fear of Crazy and need to do things differently, but are still reluctant to take action and implement real behavioral changes.

  In preparation of taking action, you examine your fears— the obstacles to saying goodbye to Crazy. Your fears may be exaggerated or quite real. After all, we are dealing with Crazy. In working through this stage, you weigh the pros and cons of changing vs. not changing. If and when you decide the pros of changing outweigh the cons, you move into the next stage.

- **Preparation.** This is the "ready to change" stage. You and your husband now have a plan in place. You bought this book. Perhaps you have hired a coach or a therapist to help and support you. Maybe you joined an online support group. You have explored and decided upon boundaries and strategies

DR. TARA PALMATIER, PSYD & PAUL ELAM

to minimize Crazy's impact on your lives. You have decided how you will respond when Crazy pushes back on your new boundaries. You also have a relapse plan in place to help you get back up on the horse when you falter, which we will discuss in Part Three of this book.

You have prepared to rid yourselves of Crazy's enablers and apologists, or decided to minimize contact with them. You have social supports in place. For when things get tough, you have set expectations and boundaries as a couple so that you do not turn on each other and in order to present a unified front to Crazy and the children. You are just about ready for the next stage.

- **Action.** As they say in the reality TV programs, for which Crazy seems to be forever auditioning, *"It's about to get real!"* You are ready to implement your strategy to say goodbye to Crazy and take action. You start your new communication plan of minimal contact. Maybe you begin the process of revising your current custody order into a parallel parenting plan, as we will discuss In Part Three. You are ready to start telling Crazy, and anyone else impeding your progress, "No."

During this stage, you will see how Crazy responds to your changes, what works, what you need to ride out and what might need some tweaking. This is an important and essential stage, but not the most important one. In our opinion, the two most important stages are Preparation and the following stage, Maintenance.

- **Maintenance.** This stage is about reinforcing and maintaining your boundaries and personal changes. Setting a boundary with Crazy once is rarely enough. She may not bang her head against your wall immediately or consistently; however, she may circle back periodically and try to encroach on your boundaries just to see if they're still in place. Yes, it's tiresome, but that's Crazy! Fortunately, it gets a lot less tiring with practice.

This stage does not require as much effort as the action stage. In the action stage, you will need to expend energy in enforcing boundaries with Crazy and yourselves. She will most likely push back at you hard, like a sumo wrestler charging at an all-you-can-eat buffet. During this stage, Crazy may still try to test your boundaries, but you will have already shown her there's a new sheriff in town, and it's not her.

- **Termination.** Oh, if one could only terminate Crazy, like a useless employee or lousy cable service. Well, you definitely can if no children are involved. Even if children are involved, you can reduce Crazy's agonizing presence in your life to a state of irrelevant nuisance.

  By the time you reach the termination stage, enforcing boundaries and thwarting Crazy's attempts to get a rise out of you are second nature, a reflex. No matter how crazy Crazy gets, you don't let it rattle you. You know how to handle your emotional responses and how to respond, or not respond to Crazy. In this respect, there is no real termination of Crazy—just maintenance until the children age out. Even then, there will be some contact with Crazy at graduations, weddings, Christenings, Bar Mitzvahs, etc.

Now that you have an understanding of change stages, where are you? Where is your husband? What needs to happen to get you both in sync? We will address these issues in the next chapter.

Takeaways

- There is a science to change. It occurs in a series of stages with which you are now familiar.

- The most profound change in you is that you switch from reacting emotionally to Crazy to reacting intellectually and with forethought. Her attempts to get under your skin result only in frustration, *for her*.

- Understanding where you and your husband each are in the change process is helpful. If one of you is ready to change and the other isn't, it can either become another source of conflict or an opportunity to help each other move to a more congruent place in the process.

Chapter 13

Getting on the Same Page

We have hammered home the fact that saying goodbye to Crazy is a team effort. In order to be successful, you and your partner must work together. Please bear with us as we flog that horse some more. The fact is that this is one point that cannot be overstated.

If you are ready to cut Crazy out of the picture, but your partner is still clinging to old behaviors such as enabling her and burying his head in the sand when it gets sticky, then before you say goodbye to Crazy you must stop first and say goodbye to old behaviors that enable Crazy.

We mean that literally. Stop.

Stop everything you are doing right now and ask yourself if you can trust your partner to fully engage with you in this process and to stand side by side with you on every decision and every strategy to put Crazy in the rearview mirror. If you don't come back with an unhesitant and unflinching *yes* to that question, then your work begins with your partner. Your work could well end there, too, if your partner is unable or unwilling to stand beside you and take the necessary actions to rid your lives of Crazy.

If he can't or won't prove himself a trustworthy ally in making this happen, it is your unfortunate task to either accept that or move on in your own best interest and in the best interests of your children. That could mean it is time for you to move on without him. We know that is an extreme, heartbreaking option. We also know that you trying to evict Crazy while he is enabling her is like walking out on a tree limb while he saws through it behind your back.

The partner who is hopelessly addicted to enabling Crazy is also actively participating in the chaos and destruction in your life. Either he gets on board with solutions, or you face some tough questions.

Are you prepared to commit to someone fully, even when it is apparent that his commitment to you is lacking and falters when it really counts? How do you feel about pulling the rug from underneath Crazy only to watch him slide a pillow under her butt just in time to cushion the fall? Do you think it is appropriate for his children to treat you with contempt and disrespect you have not earned—contempt and disrespect that was instilled by his crazy ex while he looks the other way or even asks you to tolerate it because he thinks the kids have been through too much to place normal, healthy expectations of behavior on them?

In short, are you prepared to let Crazy treat you, your children and others in your circle of care the same way that he allowed to Crazy to treat him while he was married to her and ever since?

To be blunt, if the answers to any of these questions are *yes*, you are not only participating in his lack of boundaries, you are showing that your boundaries with him are equally lacking. We understand this can be a tough pill to swallow.

This brings us to perhaps the most difficult of the proposed changes we are suggesting to your life.

Saying goodbye to Crazy means saying goodbye to all of it. That includes saying goodbye to the parts of other people who feed into Crazy, pad her corners, make excuses for her or even those who just don't have the courage to act decisively and send her packing for good.

This means Crazy's enablers and apologists, including your partner, have to go until they can convince you their ways have changed, and you should be very hard to convince.

This all boils down to you.

If, for instance, you have already decided that you want Crazy out of your life, but not at the cost of your current relationship, then you have literally opened to the door to Crazy's strategy to maintain control. She will simply take whatever pushback you send her way, punish her ex-husband with it and use it to drive a wedge between the two of you. She will win at this every time simply because your partner is willing to help her do it—and because you are not willing to insist that your relationship boundaries with anyone demand that they do not throw you under the bus just to avoid facing their own fears.

Before you say goodbye to your partner, however, there are some steps you can take to try to get your partner into the same stage of change as you. You may have already tried some of these without success. It may not hurt to try again as your husband may have inched closer to readiness since the last time you tried. Some of these things may be new. You may need to go through some of these exercises more than once or allow them some time to sink in, but not an indefinite amount of time.

Pros and cons. What's the upside to saying goodbye to Crazy, and what's the downside? Many of the cons of ridding oneself of Crazy are usually based on fear—fear of further damage to the relationship with the kids, fear of going to court or fear of false allegations. Many of your partner's fears may be legitimate. If he is not ready to take action yet, the cons will outweigh the pros. As he works through his fears, the pros should begin to outweigh the cons.

Building confidence. Crazy is to self-esteem what salt is to a garden slug. Does your partner have a case of learned helplessness? In other words, does he believe there is nothing he can do that will be effective when dealing with Crazy? Are the first words out of his mouth, "I can't," "I already tried that" or "That'll never work?" If so, he may need to do some basic goal setting work in order to rebuild his self-confidence and belief in his own personal autonomy. Instead of helping him to rebuild his confidence through taking action against Crazy, start smaller. Set achievable health and fitness goals or home improvements. Face a non-Crazy related challenge like signing up for a 5k run. If he feels more control of himself and confident in his abilities in other areas of his life, it might help him to be ready to do what is necessary to say goodbye to Crazy.

Education. Men who have been married to Crazy seem to fall into three groups—they're either self-taught experts on personality disorders or willfully ignorant. The third group are those who've managed to learn what they need to know about Crazy and have said goodbye to her. Since you're reading this book, your partner is probably in one of the first two groups. If your husband is a personality disorder expert, he may have over-analyzed himself into a state of inaction. This is what the mental health field calls *paralysis by analysis*. Over-analysis is often a form of avoidance, and a damned good one. It is the avoidance of taking necessary action by hoping that you will find another answer—an easier, less fear-inducing answer. This answer will never come, though, because it does not exist. Hopefully, reading this book will help him realize the only answer to Crazy is to strap on some boundaries and say goodbye to her.

Have you sent link after link to articles about Crazy, parental alienation and boundary setting? Does he read them, or does he reply that he finds reading this kind of information "too triggering?" If the latter is his response, he is choosing to continue to be willfully ignorant regarding the situation you are in, and that is unacceptable. He does not have to become a personality disorder expert or a legal expert, but if he truly wants Crazy out of his life, he will need to develop some expertise in moving past his fears.

Social support. Do you and your husband know other couples who have said goodbye to Crazy? Is he willing to join an online forum to communicate with others in similar situations? Sometimes, talking with other people who are in similar situations or people who were in a similar situation, but took action and improved things, can inspire us to do the same. If your partner struggles with learned helplessness, this could help him recalibrate what he believes is possible. It can also be a great way to get some moral support and feel less alone, as well as a source of information and advice. Also, publicly sharing one's goals, like saying goodbye to Crazy, increases the likelihood that you will be successful. Saying things out loud to other people has a tendency to make those things more real. This is why people share their weight loss goals, their goal to quit smoking, give up sugar and the like.

Mental health support. There are good therapists out there who can help you and your husband. You will have to do some due diligence and screen potential therapists (see *chapter 33*). You can do a combination of individual and joint sessions. Your husband may be reluctant to work with a therapist, especially if he was tag-teamed by Crazy and an enabling/apologist therapist in the past. Again, there are therapists who get it; you just have to do a little digging. Well, okay, maybe a lot—but they are out there.

Reward and punishment. Are you encouraging your husband and praising him when he enforces a boundary with Crazy? Or do you primarily focus on what he is doing wrong or not doing enough of or not doing at all? If so, it would behoove you to rethink that strategy. Nagging, even when there is abundant reason to be frustrated, is a bad practice and won't help anyone change.

You can help him prepare to take action. As we learned in basic management skills 101, people tend to respond better to positive feedback. Leadership instills more confidence than criticism. When he tells Crazy no, make him aware that you have noticed, and that you appreciate his coming through for your relationship. Remind him regularly (and feel free to be creative in how you do it) that his efforts to protect your relationship enhance your respect and admiration for him as your partner. If Crazy is going to make saying goodbye to her feel bad, you can help things along by making saying goodbye to Crazy feel really, really good!

There are other actions you can take to help get you and your partner on the same page, but these are some of the basics. Before calling it quits, we encourage you to work with your partner, keeping in mind that *he* needs to do the work. You cannot do the work for him, but you can encourage and support him in doing it. Set goals and due dates for yourselves. It may be helpful to keep a log of the items you're working on together and track your progress. It may also be helpful to do some extra reading on the processes of change and effective goal setting.

Should it become necessary to give your partner the message that either he or Crazy has to go, that you can't and won't have both in your lives, then you should consider doing it as soon as it becomes apparent that he is intractably resistant to change. If keeping him and enabling his enabling of Crazy is acceptable to you, that is your choice, of course. We strongly suggest, though, that you scrutinize that decision carefully and remain aware that it is in fact, a decision, your decision, to invite Crazy's chaos into your personal life.

We realize there will be many husbands and boyfriends reading this part of the book, as well, and we know that many will not appreciate this hardline stance. We view their position as being somewhere along the lines of a cancer patient refusing radiation and chemo because it will upset the cancer or like someone who won't quit smoking because they think the tobacco company needs the money.

The first real step is saying goodbye to Crazy is to reject crazy thinking, regardless of the source. There is no rational or emotionally healthy reason to allow Crazy to have any influence over your life.

It is up to you if what you are now getting from your partner meets your definitions of love and partnership. What will never be up to you if you make that decision, though, is whether Crazy has the master key to your personal life and the ability to create wreckage.

Bottom line, if he won't say goodbye to Crazy, or at least be willing to work on preparing himself to say goodbye to Crazy, you still can. And you must if you ever want peace in your life or a relationship with a partner who has your back. Chronic Crazy enablers don't even cover their own backs. Or their children's. Do not make the mistake of thinking they will cover yours.

Obviously, we are not here to decide if you should or should not be in a relationship. What we are saying is that your choice to live a life dominated by Crazy is your choice and your responsibility. It is not something to be blamed on him. After all, you are well aware that he has been living this way for years. So have you, and that is the problem.

Now is the time to proceed with a singular idea: one way or the other, Crazy has to go. If he reads your conviction about that correctly, he is much more likely to sign on. You must be clear, though. If this is going to work as a couple you must have his support 100%, and it must be there each and every moment. Don't accept anything less.

If he makes it necessary for you to say goodbye to Crazy on your own, then we suggest you do it. The only way is for you hand Crazy her walking papers as a team, a team that you co-captain and is a combined, inseparable force. It is up to you to start the ball rolling, and it is up to you both to keep it going.

Takeaways

- In order to say goodbye to Crazy, you and your partner must be on the same page—understanding the problem and ready, or getting ready, to take action.

- If you are not on the same page, identify the reasons why **and take action on them.**

- Prepare to help yourself and your partner get on the same page.

Chapter 14

Obstacles to Saying Goodbye to Crazy

Unfortunately, Crazy is not the only obstacle you are likely to face once you decide to say goodbye. You will likely encounter societal, cultural, religious and personal obstacles that may be more daunting than Crazy herself.

Western society is often quick to intervene when a woman is being abused and harassed by a man, but when a woman is abusing, stalking and harassing a man—well, not so much. As a woman, you may even have a hard time convincing family, friends, law enforcement and family court judges that your husband's ex and the ever-sacred mother of his children needs to receive consequences for her bad behavior, or even that there is something wrong with her behavior.

You may be told that you're just jealous and insecure that Crazy was married to and had children with your husband or boyfriend before you, or you may get cast into the role of wicked stepmother just because you fell in love with a man who had the misfortune to be ensnared by Crazy once upon a time.

Saying goodbye to Crazy can set a large part of your world against you, but the answer to that is what you might expect. Build a new world, which you can do if you are determined.

Before you implement the strategies that are discussed in Part Three, let's take a look at some of the potential obstacles you may encounter. We have divided the obstacles into cultural and personal.

Cultural Obstacles

But she's the mother of his children. This is the Golden Uterus phenomenon in full effect. As if the physical act of giving birth somehow imbues a woman with mystical, magical powers or makes her deserving of automatic respect and deference—it doesn't.

Crazy is the mother of your husband's kids. So what? That should not give her license to abuse him, violate court orders, alienate the kids, intrude in your lives and behave like an out-of-control, entitled child.

You knew what you were getting into when you married a man with kids. People who say this to you are basically telling you, "You were asking for it." It's victim blaming, and it's bullshit. With the divorce rate at over 50%, second marriages and blended families are as much a part of the cultural landscape as first marriages, and they are no less important. Indeed, your current marriage is far more relevant and important than his last one, which has already failed.

Men who marry divorced moms aren't told, "You should have known what you were getting yourself into when you married a woman with kids." If anything, men who marry divorced or single moms are viewed as saintly heroes—not home-wrecking whores who are trying to steal another man's children. Although, this is frequently happens when Crazy recouples as yet another way to hurt her ex. She makes her current victim into a shinier, newer, better *daddy du jour*—at least until she turns on him, which she most certainly will.

Marrying a divorced man with children doesn't mean you have to suffer silently and know your place. Reasonable adults with children are able to divorce, recouple and co-parent without bullying, manipulation, harassment and other forms of abuse. Both parties move on with their lives and forge a solid working relationship for the sake of the kids and are even able to be civil to each other's new significant others. This is what you should be getting yourself into when you marry a man with kids.

The best interests of the children. Divorce is rough on children. The two most important people in their lives, mom and dad, separate and life as they know it changes forever. Healthy adults keep their animosity to themselves and do what's best for their kids.

Parental conflict that continues *after* divorce is what is most damaging to children, more so than the divorce itself. In order to decrease conflict, some family, friends, judges, therapists and children's advocates believe that giving Crazy primary or sole custody and not enforcing custody order violations will appease her and reduce the conflict to which she exposes the children. Wrong, wrong, wrong. All this does is reward Crazy and incentivize more of her crazy, destructive behavior.

Crazy will also use the children as human shields and bargaining chips to extort additional money (beyond child support obligations), compliance and anything else she wants. She dresses everything up as being for "the children"—you know, the children whose father "abandoned" them. If your husband suffers from Daddy Guilt, this tactic is Crazy's ace in the hole.

Oftentimes, Crazy's children will begin to mimic their mother's behavior in order to manipulate their fathers. If this is happening with your husband's children, it needs to be nipped in the bud, which is incredibly hard for fathers who are suffering the effects of parental alienation to do.

Setting healthy boundaries with the kids is every bit as important as setting boundaries with Crazy. In fact, it's more important to set boundaries with the kids. It is one of the ways you help them *not* to follow in their mother's dysfunctional footsteps. Crazy has lived a life defined by avoiding consequences for her bad behavior and poor choices and it is a big part of the reason why Crazy is crazy.

Family Court Bias. Family courts are notoriously biased in favor of women. While this is slowly starting to shift, there's still a long, long way to go. A battle is being waged to make family court fairer and really about the best interests of the children, but it is mostly uphill and faces huge political resistance. Divorce and custody battles are a multibillion dollar a year industry. Too many attorneys see Crazy as a cash cow, not to mention the money the state generates from child support and the revenue being raked in by family court those providing ancillary service like custody evaluators, guardians ad litem, and visitation supervision centers. These people are the family court equivalent of ticks, and once embedded they're very hard to remove.

Mental Health Bias. There is an incredible female bias in the mental health field as well. Some of Crazy's biggest enablers are therapists. Even therapists who see that Crazy is the problem will enable her for the revenue source or because it's easier to have you and your husband modify your behaviors and keep taking the hits, than it is to stand up to Crazy and hold her accountable.

Personal Obstacles

Family of origin issues. People who get involved with Crazy or have difficulty enforcing boundaries with Crazy often have some family of origin issues that groomed them to be targets for Crazy. Common issues include being a people pleaser, being an approval seeker, being shame-based, having a fear of conflict and confrontation, being a rescuer-fixer-hero, a need to be needed, a need to be liked and a vulnerability to fear, obligation and guilt. Fear, obligation and guilt are Crazy's most frequently used weapons and compliance tactics. Additionally, if you or your husband has a Crazy for a parent, this behavior may be seen as normal or as something that is unavoidable and to just be tolerated.

Daddy Guilt. Daddy Guilt is one of the biggest obstacles to overcome when saying goodbye to Crazy. It is so problematic that it is discussed in its very own chapter, *chapter 17.*

Religious or faith community. There are faiths that advise men it is their responsibility to remain in a marriage no matter how abusive their spouse is or blame them for their spouse's behavior. Some religious leaders tell men they are failing in their role of husband if their wives behave like Crazy. If your husband is vulnerable to guilt, obligation and shaming tactics, your faith community may very well be an obstacle to saying goodbye to Crazy.

Mental health issues. If your husband suffers from anxiety or depression, this could be another stumbling block. Depression can lead to feelings of learned helplessness and vice versa. Learned helplessness causes an individual to believe that no matter what he or she does it will fail, so why bother trying. Anxiety can heighten the fears surrounding setting boundaries with Crazy. Individuals with ADHD, Asperger's and other neurodiversity issues are also especially vulnerable to Crazy. They are often quick to take on blame and, because they can be very literal, will continue to believe Crazy even though she has a history of being dishonest and manipulative.

Lack of personal resolve. What can also hurt you immensely is a failing of your own resolve. Politely asking your partner if they would please stop throwing you under the bus is, quite frankly, a poor way to stay out from under the bus. So is pleading with them to do the right thing. Boundaries don't just apply to Crazy. They apply to everyone.

One possible reason that your efforts to enlist his help may have failed in the past is because he may not be taking you seriously. To be even more frank, if he is not taking you seriously, it may be in part because you are not taking yourself seriously.

Is it okay to throw you under the bus, to betray your trust, because he is afraid of his ex-wife? If it is not okay, then the onus is on you to prove it. Loyalty is not something anyone should have to beg for in a relationship. Loyalty, like fidelity and other deal breakers, is something you go into a relationship *insisting* on without remorse or compunction.

We suggest that, rather than ask your partner not to throw you under the bus, you simply advise him that any relationship which leaves tread marks on your back is a relationship you will not endure.

If every other good faith attempt you have made to enlist your partner's help has failed, do not hesitate to inform him that a lack of loyalty won't be tolerated. We know that is a tough, even grueling call, but it is also the very mentality you must cultivate when it comes to dealing with Crazy and her enablers. Anything else is a waste of time. Enough of your time has already been wasted.

Some of these obstacles are insurmountable. You won't be able to change the cultural and religious beliefs of many individuals and institutions. However, the obstacles that are of your own making or unresolved childhood issues are well within your power to change.

Takeaways

- There are many obstacles to putting Crazy in her proper perspective vis-a-vis your life. Cultural, social, legal, mental health, your respective families—all of these can and will combine forces to shut you up and to bury your very real issues under their *concern* for Crazy. You don't need to accept that.

- You cannot change most of forces that enable Crazy. That's okay. You don't need to.

- Change yourself and your spouse in the ways needed for the betterment of YOUR family. Let the naysayers and critics fall to the wayside where they belong. They do not have to deal with Crazy in the same ways you do.

Chapter 15

A Letter to Husbands and Boyfriends

Greetings Gents,

Okay, so you have just been handed this to read by your wife or girlfriend. That most likely means that your ex-wife or former girlfriend has been causing problems in your life. Those problems have probably persisted long after your marriage or relationship ended.

Maybe your ex is still bitter over your marriage or over your divorce or break-up. Maybe she does not like your new partner and tries to meddle in your new life. Perhaps she is dragging your children into it, and they are disrespecting your partner or you, or both. It is possible she uses the courts or your visitation rights to cause problems.

Whatever she is doing it is enough of a pain in the neck that your partner has been putting pressure on you to do something about it. In fact, part of that pressure is handing this to you to read.

How are we doing so far?

If none of this is ringing true, if you are 100% sure that it does not fit your life in any way, then congratulations, you can quit reading. Just hand this book back to your partner and feel secure in the knowledge that she is just seeing things that don't exist.

But if this applies to you, please read on. We have some things to say that may be of help.

First, let's just forget about your partner for just a moment. The fact is that we're not writing this to grab you by the collar on her behalf. In the end, this is about you. It is about your future, your happiness, your children (if you have them) and your relationship with them. So let's start with some questions that are about you.

Does your ex-wife cause problems in your life? It is a simple and straightforward question. Is she continuing her desire to control, punish or get retribution against you because she feels like you failed in your relationship with her? Is she manipulating you or trying to manipulate you for financial or other forms of support?

Has she warmed up to calling the shots in as many places in your life as possible? Does she have you constantly measuring your words—biting your tongue—in your interactions with her? Are you frequently afraid of how your conflicts with her may affect your children? Are you worried about her taking her complaints to her attorney?

Have your children begun to disrespect you? Have they taken to viewing you in much the same way that she does, as a loser whose wallet is pried open with guilt trips and other forms of manipulation?

This does lead us back to your partner for a moment. Have your children begun to disrespect her or her children? Have her children started picking up bad habits?

Now for the most important question of all. If any, or all of this, actually describes your life, what are you doing to put a stop to it?

Note that when we ask this we are not asking what you are doing to survive it. We are not asking how you go about trying to keep the peace despite her endless efforts to create chaos and disharmony. We are not asking what you do to avoid problems so they won't affect the kids.

What you are doing to stop your ex's continued efforts to trash your life? We ask this for a good reason—the number of men who go through this with crazy exes are as countless as the stars.

Most of them just lie down and take it.

Some men in your position develop strategies to try to reduce the damage, most of which amount to hiding out, tolerating intolerable behavior, and gagging themselves so the ex doesn't get mad and make things worse. Most focus on keeping the peace more than actually stopping the insanity. They rationalize with excuses like "she is the mother of my children," and "if I set limits with her or tell her no it will only make things worse."

They come up with these and many other excuses for living life as a doormat, and most of them suffer for it. They lose the respect of their children, which can and does lead to estrangement. They find that many times, one after another, any attempts they make to find any sort of happiness in a relationship are undermined by the crazy ex, who just won't permit their former partners to find happiness with anyone else.

Unfortunately, most of these men sit back, do nothing and allow it to happen.

Their losses from that are understandable. Few people, even with the supposed lifelong bond of parent and child, are going to remain interested in a relationship with someone they don't respect. It is just a reality of human interaction. The same holds true for romantic involvements. How long will anyone honestly stay with someone they don't respect or who does not have the will to insist that others treat them with respect? How long will anyone be trusted who will tolerate anything, even the alienation of their own children, just so they don't have to face a woman's wrath? Why should anyone trust them?

How secure and loved will anyone feel with someone like this?

We know these are tough questions. And as we said, if they don't apply to you then you need not have wasted your time even reading this far. But man, if this is you, you can and should be doing something about it. Not for her, and not even necessarily for your kids. Certainly it is not for your ex. It is for you.

Don't you owe it to yourself not to live your life on a leash, causing the people in your life to see you as a walked dog?

Don't get us wrong. This is not about your manhood. The fact is that everyone in a relationship has an obligation to protect that relationship. Women can fail at this as much as men. Your partner has the same obligations you do about keeping destructive people out of the picture. It's about your happiness. And that, quite frankly, is in your hands, whether you know it or not.

Before we continue, let us assure you that we get it. If you have a history with a high-conflict woman who has become the nightmare that just won't go away, the last thing you may feel you need is anyone, including your wife—and least of all strangers like us—pointing the finger at you and causing you more grief than you're already dealing with.

We have written this book specifically to help you and your partner deal more effectively with the lunatic who has had too much power in your life, and who has had too much of a negative impact on your relationships, with each other and with your children if you have them.

There are workable solutions. There may not be a way to solve every problem 100%, and we can certainly not guarantee that she will never cause you any problems again, but we do know that in most cases serious improvement is possible.

If your case is like most, serious improvement is desperately needed.

The thing is that it absolutely requires you and your partner working together as a unified team to make it happen. That is why we wrote this letter to you, and why you have been asked to read it.

A crazy ex can be a tsunami of trouble that just keeps hitting the beach, over and over again, wiping out everything in its path. They get you right where it hurts any time they want, and many of them want to do so very badly. If you have children with this kind of woman, that problem only becomes worse and a lot more complicated, because she uses her position as the mother of your children to wield power over you and anyone close to you. If you are in that situation you know the courts will back her and you know that she damned well knows that too.

But here is the deal. If your ex is causing problems, if she is pitting your children against you and/or your partner, if she is instigating conflict between your children and your partner's children or if she is causing harm to your relationship, then it is up to the adults in your relationship to do what it takes to put a stop to it.

That means you and your partner. If your partner thinks that the idea here is for you to mount a white horse and ride in to the rescue, then we would advise her to read this book again until she understands that this is not about getting you to be *the man*. The only way this works, the only way you will find solutions, is with the two of you together on equal footing.

The fact that you have been asked to read this should be telling you that you have a concerned partner who wants to do something about this problem. Whether you do, of course, is entirely up to you. But please be aware that any denial you want to maintain about what is happening is a luxury that can come with a very heavy cost.

If you are prepared to bow your head or be a punching bag for the next several years, be our guest. But allow us to respectfully suggest the costs associated with that very poor choice, including the faith and respect of your partner, will be no one's fault but your own.

Also, if you are going to abandon your responsibility to teach your children respect, healthy communication and boundaries, then you may well be condemning them to ultimately live through the same kinds of problems you are living through now. We acknowledge that is a very rough thing to say, but we won't pretend it is not true to spare your feelings.

We believe there are solutions throughout this book that can help you and your partner say good-bye to the Crazy that has taken over so much of your life. We are not pretending it's easy or that it won't require some very tough decisions, but if you have any interest in at all in facing this thing head on, please take our suggestion and start reading this book from page one. Start learning about the nature of the problems you are facing, and how to deal with them in an entirely different way. Join with your partner and work together on getting your lives back.

Takeaways

- If your ex-wife is currently having a negative impact on your relationship with your wife or girlfriend, then you should read the rest of this book.

- If your partner sees enough of a problem that you were asked to read this chapter, be mindful that your relationship could be, for better or worse, reaching a turning point.

- If your children are treating you or your partner with disrespect, allowing that to happen is preparing them for a lifetime of their own failed relationships.

Chapter 16

A Letter to Wives and Girlfriends

You can say no to almost anything that you're asked to do.
You can say no. You can say no way, or you can say no thank you.
You can reject a final request, and deny a desperate plea.
You can say no when they ask you to agree to surgery.
Almost every single time, negativity will pull you through, but you're in a mess when she wants a yes because she'll get it right out of you.
Cause you can't say no. No, no, no, to that woman.
(Loudon Wainwright, III)

Greetings Ladies,

There is a good deal of truth to these song lyrics. And while we have no desire to make light of your circumstances or your partner's, this bit of humorous songwriting makes a good launching point for us to have a discussion about men.

It is a necessary discussion. Many women reading this book have in common husbands or boyfriends who can't or won't be assertive enough with Crazy to put an end to the problems she causes. In talking with many women in this position, we have found a common theme of frustration—that he is not stepping up to protect the relationship he started. He is not ensuring that both he and his partner are treated with respect by Crazy and often by the children he has with her, and that he is indeed like that song—caving in situation by situation, year after year to the same person, and that he is doing little or nothing to stop it from happening.

He is a man who may be strong and in control in every other area of his life, but when it concerns dealing with his ex, he weakens to the point of looking like another person entirely—a stranger who cannot muster a simple *no* for any reason.

If this sounds painfully familiar, your feelings are not off the mark. With many, many men who have been through a marriage or long-term relationship with a high-conflict, abusive personality, this is a fair characterization of how they handle things, which is to say they don't handle things at all. They tend look for ways to appease and keep the peace, and sometimes they simply withdraw and pretend it isn't happening. They do so at the unfortunate expense of their current relationship, and even to the detriment of their parenting.

It is important for you to know how things got to this point if you are going to be able to do anything about it. What may surprise you is that your partner not standing up for himself is not just about the crazy ex.

It has everything to do with men and how we shape masculinity in this society.

Understanding this requires us to examine aspects of masculinity that most of us are very rarely asked to consider. For the most part, our culture teaches us that men are powerful. In fact, if you listen to people like feminist ideologues you will very often hear that men are *too* powerful, that they thrive on control and domination, and that women in particular have long suffered for it.

Like the song lyrics there is perhaps a shadow of truth to this. Moving out of that shadow and into the light, however, we find a different story.

We certainly *expect* men to be powerful. The expectation of strength and control is hammered into men from birth, from parents, society, media, peers, other men and very, very importantly, from women. Personal power and strength are the kinds of things that make men attractive to women. Despite what we are led to believe by magazines like Cosmo and most self-help literature, a man's strength and self-confidence is how most women will measure his masculine appeal—not his sensitivity or ability to express his feelings in a feminine way.

Without his masculine strength, he risks rejection and solitude. Weak men, men who cannot take care of themselves and others, do not expect the opportunity for love and companionship from women. Men who get in touch with their feminine side also tend to get in touch with sleeping alone.

It may not be politically correct to say so, but that does not make it any less true.

Fair or not, strength is what makes men loveable. Strength ultimately defines, at least in the minds of most men, their ultimate worth as human beings. We are not talking about an inconsequential matter here. We are talking about literally everything that makes men feel valuable and worthwhile.

Right now, for you, it is your partner's lack of strength that is the source of a lot of your pain and frustration.

Why, one must wonder, would a man so rigidly trained to value personal power and strength falter when it comes to asserting themselves with Crazy?

He has been socialized to value and pursue the characteristics of strength and personal power because they are essential elements in making him a good protector and provider—*for women*. In other words, the strength we expect of him is the strength required to give women what they want and need. His failure to do that is his failure as a man, at least in his mind.

In that light, the simple act of saying no, which may appear to you to be a simple, obvious choice, is not so simple and obvious in the mind of your partner.

We ask you to consider him and other men you have known who have gone through divorce and/or breakups. Did they fight tooth and nail to win, or did they try to get through the experience with as little uproar as possible, often making sacrificial concessions just to avoid fighting?

Did they scrape and claw to keep assets, use the children as pawns, or did they just try to survive, looking, often futilely, for a peaceful, amicable dissolution of the marriage?

Of course there are exceptions, but as a rule our experience with men going through a hostile divorce is that they not only want, more than anything, for things to be resolved as smoothly as possible, but they are often so dedicated to that line of thinking that they cannot entertain the idea of taking off the gloves and fighting, even for basic fairness.

Many of them struggle to the end with the idea of the marriage ending and live in denial about it, regardless of how bad things have become. They go through the divorce hoping that their conciliatory ways will prevent the inescapable end.

Because of all these things, they often lose. Badly.

We are betting that for you, some or all of this describes the divorce or breakup of your current partner.

We realize this view of things can be unsettling. It is important, however, to understand precisely what it is your partner has to overcome in order to take an effective, lasting stand against Crazy. Namely, he has to dismiss a lifetime of programming that tells him he is not a man if he puts his needs ahead of those of a woman.

To flatly reject the stated "needs" of a woman, even highly irrational and unreasonable ones, particularly from a woman with whom he shares children, or with whom he has been in a long term relationship, is more difficult for most men than you might imagine. On some level, it is a rejection of their masculine programming, a failure that will bring them deep shame.

They just can't say no to that woman.

Men are never given tools or education about how to defend themselves with women or even informed that they should. It is just the opposite. They are trained, and quite brutally, that conflict with a woman in which they fight back in any way, is the act of a bully and a coward, not a man. It doesn't matter how justified they are, or even how important it really is that they defend themselves. To do so is a betrayal of what they have been trained to believe manhood is about.

This is something about which Crazy is instinctively aware. She is an expert at manipulating compliance from a man. She has learned every one of your partner's buttons and how to push them skillfully, and often at will. She can make him feel small and guilty and wrong at any given moment. She has been doing it for years.

As this story illustrates, and as elements of your life with your current partner may also confirm, what he needs more than anything is incentive and the correct kind of pressure from you to hold his ground, with your conscious understanding of how difficult and stressful it may be for him to do so. It is something he is unlikely to do on his own. His conditioning as a man, compounded with a history of her shaming and abuse, drives him to act in her interest over his own, even when it also has consequences for the people he loves.

He needs support to move toward taking care of himself and his relationship with you, and he frankly needs the occasional kick in the pants to get results. It is important to remember, though, that this is not a tug-of-war between you and Crazy with him as the rope. It is not just about getting him to say yes to you instead of her.

This brings us to another point, and likely to a more targeted description of your frustrations. His inability to say no is limited to his dealings with her. The thing that compounds your problems is that he caves in to her, puts up with her abuse and even puts up with abuse from the children they share, but when you demand that he take a stand for your relationship he folds like a cheap suit. *He chooses to tolerate her shenanigans instead of fulfilling his commitments as your partner.*

You appear to be the only one with which he can take a stand, the only one he can deny, and for all the wrong reasons. It is a disappointing and often painful betrayal of the loyalty you brought to the relationship.

So, this may leave you asking, "Well, if this stuff is really rooted in his sense of manhood, then why is he choosing to be like that with her instead of me? Why does Crazy get his cooperation, and I don't?"

In almost all cases it is not because he cares about her more than he cares about you. It is because she has learned to manipulate and bully him and has established a long-term pattern of getting her way, no matter what. She warmed up to calling the shots with him a long time before he ever met you. With her he is simply doing what he is used to doing, what he has been trained to do with a particular person for a long time.

The fact that you are not Crazy ironically works against you, in a way. Simply speaking, it is safer to say no to a sane person than it is to a crazy person. He may even be more willing to fight back with you than he is with her. If that's true, it is likely because fighting back with you doesn't mean the same kind of insanity that Crazy has always made sure he suffered for denying her wishes. You are safer than Crazy, so you are more likely to end up being the one to whom he says no, or sadly, the one he ignores.

Again, he is in all likelihood not making conscious choices. He is not actively deciding that he is going to pick her over you. He is just following a pattern of behavior that has been established over a prolonged period.

Breaking free of that habit is not easy. That is okay. By the time you finish following the advice in this book, you will both do many things that are not easy. All of them will strengthen you, strengthen your relationship and put you closer to your goal of a Crazy-free life.

Let's be clear about this, though. If you are going to say good-bye to Crazy, your partner's tolerant ways with her are going to have to end. It is very simple: you can't show Crazy the door if he is undermining you and standing in the way. You and your partner absolutely must work together to solve this problem. And by solve we mean a complete or near complete removal of Crazy from your lives.

The trick is in how you get there. Now, if you want the cheap and easy way, you can just use what already works on him. You can shame him, undermine his self-respect, push and coerce him into choosing you over her. You can shame his manhood, make him feel inferior and wrong ever chance you get till you get your way.

In other words, you can become Crazy.

Problem is, he ended up with you because a bad ending is where a relationship with Crazy leads, at least for those that are lucky. In the long run, Crazy's way is a dead end. Crazy's way is the problem you are trying to solve, not a solution you want to emulate. And besides, Crazy is not just in what you do, it is in who you are. If you are not Crazy, as a person, it will be very difficult for you to use her ways effectively.

You need something else—something lasting, and something that works—especially when it comes to getting him to make the transition from Crazy's enabler to the man who hands her an eviction notice. We are going to break that down for you after we explore some more obstacles to saying goodbye to Crazy.

Takeaways

- Your partner struggles with Crazy precisely because men are programmed not to fight back against women.

- In addition, he has personally learned that going against Crazy brings very negative consequences.

- He stands up to you rather than her because you are sane, and thus, safer than Crazy.

- He can learn how to stand up to her even with negative consequences. He will need your support as he learns new habits in relation to dealing with her.

Chapter 17

Daddy Guilt:
Divorce Means Having to Say
You're Sorry Forever

In the first chapter of this book, we told you that divorce and bitterness go together like gasoline and matches. Actually, that is true about divorce and many other emotions. The breakup of a long-term relationship unfortunately engenders a wide spectrum of negative feelings: anger, sadness, anxiety, and, in the experience of most people, guilt.

During a divorce, especially those that involve children, we feel guilt for a lot of reasons. We feel guilty for the trauma that children experience seeing their parents take the nuclear option of breaking up the home, for altering the course of their lives in a way that for many children is unimaginable until it happens and for taking the kind of stability that only two parents under one roof can provide.

When it comes to the children, it is not just a marriage, but also an entire family that is coming to an end. It gives the expression "Mom and Dad," a different, emotionally charged and often heartbreaking meaning. It means their lives will literally never be the same again. And it breeds a sense of guilt that many fathers, especially non-custodial ones, have a difficult time coming to grips with.

You can be assured that Crazy knows this and uses it to her advantage. She will use it to foster conflict in her ex-husband's new home, to extort agreement and cooperation from him on everything from money to visitation and to control him whenever he attempts to set a limit or say no.

As tough as divorce is, it is something children can and do survive, and they even ultimately flourish if they have two parents who refuse to allow the end of their marriage become the end of their children's security and sense of well-being.

But, when you add Crazy into that mix, it goes from what should be a painful but manageable transition in their lives, to a permanent pattern of sadistic, repetitive destruction and abuse that can leave them permanently and irrevocably scarred.

Embittered, high conflict ex-wives don't try to help children regroup, heal and move on after the divorce. They don't try to restructure the family in a way that serves the interest of the children. They just add the kids to the arsenal of weapons, who in turn become more cannon fodder in her escalating war against the father. This describes Crazy to a tee. She uses his Daddy Guilt, twisting it and inflating it opportunistically. Crazy teaches the children to do it as well, often using them to work in concert with her destructive plans. It's her way to slide the knife in and keep twisting, over and over again.

It works like gangbusters. And when the guilt is running like a well-oiled machine, it also becomes one of the primary sources of conflict and disharmony in his new relationship.

Many of the second wives we have spoken with have confirmed this as a major source of friction in their marriage. His constant yielding to unreasonable demands and tolerance of inappropriate behavior, all driven by a toxic form of guilt, makes his loyalty to himself and his new family appear questionable.

Frequently his children will treat his new wife or partner with benign indifference, or outright disrespect, which he will tolerate under the auspices of "Oh, they have been through so much. Give them time, they will come around."

Wrong. It will become a pattern that persists for years, even to the point that it is normalized in the new family.

It is important to keep in mind that the children are frequently also being driven by guilt. Crazy lets them know, either with glaring directness, or tacit manipulation, that warming up to their stepmother is a betrayal against her. Often they will even like Dad's new partner, but will feel compelled to be distant or abrasive because they are afraid it will hurt or *anger* their mother. And when Mom is Crazy, they are right to have that fear.

We will cover what to do about this in the latter part of this book, but it is important for now to say that doing something is essential. Tolerating disrespect of the father's chosen partner, whether rooted in anger over the divorce, or a convoluted and manipulated sense of loyalty to the biological mother, is a severe and often lethal blow to the trust in a relationship. It is, in reality, colluding with Crazy by helping her drive a wedge in the new relationship and between father and child. Allowing it to pass, for any reason, is a mistake.

It is also important to understand that while guilt over what divorce does to children is a given, yielding to it and allowing it to interfere with good parenting, is ultimately a problem rooted in selfishness.

By this we don't mean the same type of selfishness that would drive a mother to instruct her children to disrespect their father or his new wife, but it is selfishness just the same.

By sacrificing normal, healthy limits fathers put on the conduct of their children out of a sense of guilt, the father is actually taking care of his emotions at the expense of his children. He is trading off his responsibility to instill respect and values in his children in exchange for a temporary and insincere bit of approval, or to keep the peace. You see, not only will his children not appreciate hearing him set limits or say no, Crazy can and will go ballistic over it.

In this respect, *keeping the peace with the children* is often code speak for continuing to bow to the will of his ex-wife. It is the excuse he uses for allowing her to continue to pull the strings in his new life, which of course means it really isn't his life at all. It's *hers*.

The more we look at "Daddy Guilt," the more we see that it is not so much an emotion as it is a weapon. It is used to bludgeon everything from his self-respect, to the respect of his children, to his authority as a father, and to his new marriage. The result is children who are robbed of needed discipline from a father they will invariably see as weak and impotent. Just like Crazy wants them to.

When there are stepsiblings involved, it can even get more complicated and damaging. These children often end up seeing the father's children live by different rules than the ones that govern their home lives. Where compliance with the rules of the home is expected from them, they see permissiveness extended to his children. They watch the father's children disrespect their mother, and they watch their stepfather tolerate it. They too, will lose respect for him, and it will destabilize their sense of security in the home.

All so Dad doesn't have to feel guilty about a divorce that he likely did not cause in the first place. When this happens, Crazy's reach into the home is all but complete.

Takeaways

- Divorce brings guilt on the part of all sane parents. Feeling that guilt is normal. Abandoning your sensibilities as a parent or a partner because of that guilt is its own problem, and a profound one.

- Stop reacting out of guilt, fear, anger, and misguided obligation, and you automatically disarm Crazy.

- It's Dad's job to stop Crazy from weaponizing what is initially a normal, healthy part of the grief process.

- Children can and do survive divorce as long as their parents are committed to ensuring their continued security in spite of changing family dynamics.

- As Crazy will not be doing that, Dad must be the parent who does.

- Dad must insist on boundaries for the children, as well as for Crazy. To do otherwise allows the children to carry his burdens. That is not appropriate. Since Crazy will never step up for the kids, Dad must be the one to do so, even if it is difficult and painful. Nobody ever said being a good parent was easy.

Chapter 18

Stepmom Guilt:
This Ain't the Brady Bunch

In the previous chapter, we discuss Daddy Guilt. Now we are going to discuss an even more taboo topic—Stepmom Guilt—because stepmoms are people, too. (Quick! Someone get a tranquilizer gun for the Golden Uteri reading this!) While this chapter is written specifically for the stepmoms, whether you're technically married or not, it will be helpful for the dads to read as well. Our society typically lauds men who marry single mothers. Stepdads are often viewed as heroes, deservedly or undeservedly. Meanwhile stepmoms are usually viewed as child stealers and jealous hags. Neither stereotype is particularly accurate.

When your husband has children with a crazy ex, the guilt, anger and other feelings and issues you, the stepmom, feel are often ignored, belittled or minimized. We have found in our work with couples who deal with Crazy, that the stepmom is usually the last person to be addressed in terms of needs or wants, that is, if her needs and wants are considered at all.

Historically, stepmoms have gotten a bad rap. Looking at world mythologies and fairy tales, the stepmother is the "wicked stepmother," shows favoritism to her own children or murders her stepchildren, so her children will inherit wealth or the throne. In stories as far back as we can remember, the stepmothers are portrayed as people who hate the fact that the man had a life, a wife and children before she came along. Tales of how stepmothers try—and usually fail—to remove the past from their husbands' lives abound.

You can toss all that garbage out the window right now.

In our experience, stepmoms, particularly stepmoms whose husbands share children with Crazy, struggle with several common issues. Whether you're cast as the home-wrecking whore, child thief, wicked, jealous, etc., being stepmom to the offspring of the Golden Uterus is typically a less than thankless job. It is far worse when your husband neither supports nor protects your role as his wife.

You Are Not Their Mom!

How often have you heard this? While there are stepmoms who try to push the biological mother out of the picture, most stepmoms don't get married in order to mother other peoples' children. Most women who marry want to be married to that man. They *do* want to be respected and treated as the other responsible adult in their home. But mother another woman's child?

Most stepmoms say *no thank you*. The myth persists, however, that if you marry a man with a child, or children, you are doing so in order to steal the children of his ex-wife. More often than not, this is about Crazy's five fears . If the children grow to like, admire or, dare we say, *love* you it triggers Crazy's fears of abandonment, loss of control, feelings of inferiority or inadequacy and her public persona of being mother of the year.

There is often an attitude of, "You may have stolen my man, but you will not steal my children!" This one is a bit difficult to comprehend especially if Crazy initiated divorce proceedings against your husband, or if you didn't meet your husband until long after he was separated or divorced. But then, as we have amply demonstrated in this book, the only reality Crazy typically does is reality TV.

Believing stepmoms desire to steal children is ultimately an absurd idea. Having a child is relatively easy, therefore, there's no reason to "steal" a child. Only Crazy sees the children as a thing to be stolen. If one wishes to have a child, one doesn't even need a man. Taking on children who have a mother present, particularly Crazy, is no one's dream.

We strongly encourage you not to take on this guilt trip. While society lauds men who marry divorced women with children, the same is not true for second wives and stepmoms. Your response to this emotionally charged and faulty assertion is simple: "No, I am not their mom, nor do I want to be. They have two parents. I am not one. I will, however, not be treated as anything less than the other adult in my home, nor will I be treated with disrespect or hatefulness." Such a statement removes a lot of the nonsense that goes along with the rallying cry of how you, the stepmom, are not the mom.

Treat your Stepchildren as your Own

Ah, the contradictions of Crazy. They never end, do they? You are *not* their mother, BUT you had better treat your stepchildren as if they were your own. If you buy your children iPads, you need to buy your step-kids iPads, too—even if they already have iPads from their maternal grandparents. Taking your kids to Disney? Don't even think about leaving the steps behind, even if they've already gone to Disney twice this year with their mother's side of the family, and Crazy will not accommodate your travel dates. That just shows how much you hate your stepchildren, you cold, hard-hearted Hannah!

Thus begins the wicked stepmother perp walk and apology tour. If you do not treat them like your children, no matter how poorly they treat you (which is deserved, as you're not their mom) you are a bad person and an awful stepmom.

It's a vicious circle. You cannot win with such social mores no matter what you do.

You do not have to treat the stepchildren as your own. If you do, if you love them like your own, good for you! We believe wholeheartedly that any stepparent can love their stepchildren as their own, but it is not required. It's a bonus.

What you must do is treat them respectfully and with kindness. If they do not respond in kind, like with anyone else who does not treat you appropriately, you are within your rights and living up to your responsibilities to insist on boundaries and proportionate consequences.

The Children You Have with your Spouse Aren't as Important

We hear this as well. The "first" children are the ones who matter.

Bullshit, is what we say. All your spouse's children matter. No children matter more than others. If your spouse has four children, two with Crazy and two with you, then he has four children, all of whom are equally important to him.

Overcoming this ideal is a tough one. The courts, the mental health industry, society, etc., have all bought into the myth of "the first family." The only First Family is in the White House, as far as we know. There is no first or second family. Your spouse has however many children he has. They are all important. *To him.*

This also means that it's okay for you to put *your* kids first. If you have children from a previous relationship, as well as with your spouse, you as their parent put them first. This also means it's okay to put them before your stepchildren.

Why? Your stepchildren have two parents. Neither of whom is you. It's up to their parents to meet their needs. Don't fall victim to taking care of the stepchildren over anyone else, including taking care of yourself. Besides, if your steps treat you like the hired help and expect you to kiss their behinds, what are you teaching them if you comply? You're most likely reinforcing the Crazy that is modeled by their mother. Don't do it.

Children of Divorce

So often, we see the children of Crazy given preference over any other children that may be in the home, and over the needs and desires of everyone else. Why? Because they are children of divorce.

The children of divorce are the very most special-est of the special-est snowflakes. If the children of divorce behave like entitled, rude brats, the prevailing mentality seems to be that you must look the other way and tolerate it because their parents are *divorced*. And it's probably somehow your fault, too!

The steps don't let you know that they're coming to see their father over the weekend until the last possible minute? Well you're just a big old meanie if you don't drop all your plans, which you tried to include them in earlier in the week via email and they ignored, and accommodate their last minute decision to notify their father that they will be gracing you with their presence. That's proof that you are a bad person who is controlling their father. The steps want extra money for one more extracurricular activity that they're going to lose interest in and drop out of because Crazy is too lazy to drive them to and from and make sure that they practice that you and your husband can ill afford? That's proof positive that their father loves *you* and *your* children more.

This is especially irksome when your husband caters to his children's bad behavior and sense of entitlement—usually due to Daddy Guilt.

It is the parents' responsibility to make sure their children are emotionally well-adjusted before, during and after divorce. If they are not your children, it is not your responsibility. If they are your stepchildren, in your home, it's your spouse's responsibility to make that happen.

Just Say No

One of the most difficult things to do as a stepmom is to say no.

This is another boundary issue—*your boundaries*. Just like we told your husband in the chapter on Daddy Guilt, it is healthy and necessary for a parent to have boundaries with his or her children whether they're divorced or not.

What are your boundaries with your step-kids? With your husband? With Crazy (if you have to interact with her)? What are you willing to tolerate? What will you not tolerate from him and his kids? What lines must not be crossed? Have you had this conversation with your husband yet? Have you had this conversation with the steps?

Healthy families have expectations for appropriate behavior and rules—intact families and blended families alike. It is a bit trickier with blended families because the two households may very well have different rules, expectations and codes of conduct. If Crazy heads one of the households, your stepchildren could very well be bouncing between Crazy's version of *Lord of the Flies* and a home that fosters respect, a good work ethic, love and shared responsibility. It could very well be a schizoid experience for your stepchildren.

Nevertheless, you want to help your partner. You want to make things easier for the kids. Contrary to popular opinion, most stepmoms are predisposed to like and welcome their stepchildren. You want to create a family with you and your spouse as the cornerstones, and allow for all members to be happy.

This means you'll say yes a lot when you'd rather say no. Especially when the kids say, "But mom lets us . . ." or "At mom's house we can . . ." or "Mom says we don't have to . . ." That's when your husband or you say, "Different house. Different rules." This is not a foreign concept to kids who most certainly observe different rules at school, in their friends' homes, at church, in other family members' homes, etc.

Then, there's Crazy. Crazy is a master at asking you to do things for her, and then punishing you for it. We hear from a lot of stepmoms who say that Crazy is happy to have them do the running around or the grunt work, and then tell the stepmom in the next breath she can't show up for the school play or the basketball game. By the way, this is often a rookie mistake stepmoms make. You think you're marrying the *Brady Bunch*, but instead you get the *Crazy Bunch*.

So, learn to say no.

Say no to your spouse, because *he* is the parent of these children. While it may make it easier for him, in the long run, the kids want their dad. It's normal. He's their parent. They may like you, but he's their parent.

Say no to Crazy. She is not your friend, and she is not family. She is someone who will knife you in the back the second you even think of turning away from her. You owe her nothing.

Say no to your stepchildren. If you would tell your own children no, it's okay to tell your stepchildren no. If you would chastise your children for misbehaving or acting out, you can set the same limits with your stepchildren.

The key for you, the stepmom, is to treat your stepchildren with kindness and decency, and to expect that in return. And, when you have to see Crazy, be civil without being a doormat.

In fact, try not to see Crazy at all. You did not marry her or have children with her. Frankly, she is really not your burden to carry. That is on your spouse. Other than civility, Crazy has no demands she can make of you. You have no obligation to her whatsoever.

Takeaways

- You matter. If your stepchildren are cruel, hostile or disrespectful, you have a right and an obligation to yourself to force a change.

- You and your husband both have an obligation to your relationship to reject abusive treatment from either of your children, his kids and your kids.

- You don't have to treat your stepchildren as if they're your own, however, there shouldn't be two sets of rules, one for your kids and another for his.

- It's okay if you and your step-kids don't become super close, but you can and should expect to treat one another with civility and respect.

Chapter 19

The Theory and Practice of Bringing the Pain

So far we have gone over ample reasons why it is important, even vital, to say good-bye to Crazy. We have covered why terminating or vastly reducing contact is a much better option than trying to negotiate, placate or maneuver Crazy into being more manageable or sane. Hopefully, at this point, you don't need convincing that Crazy is an unsalvageable mess, because if you do, then you likely have problems with which this book cannot help you.

Pardon the bluntness. It isn't intended to be insulting, but as we have promised from the beginning, we are not here to sugar coat the truth or to participate in any denial about what you're dealing with. The only solution to Crazy is to say goodbye to her in every way you possibly can. Only then can you begin to move on with your life having greatly diminished or eliminated her destructive influence on it.

Saying goodbye isn't particularly easy, and it can be quite complicated, but it is completely do-able in most cases provided you are committed, above all else, to making it happen. In fact, if you make eliminating Crazy from your life as important as it deserves to be, it will be very difficult for you to fail, even if those around you falter and cave in.

Getting there will require a fundamental understanding of what makes human beings tick, especially with each other. Remember, fundamental does not mean easy. It just means basic, and basics are where we are going to start, with a simple, inescapable rule that governs most human interaction.

In life, we tend to get from other people what we tolerate from them.

This inescapable truth is at the heart of your present circumstances, and there is no way to overcome it without accepting that truth and acting accordingly. If we are honest with ourselves, we find that in most situations as adults where people mistreated us, or who looked the other way as we were mistreated, that we, at the very least, participated in our own problems by tolerating it, by failing to set limits and by failing to have standards in relationships from which we don't retreat.

Are there exceptions to this? Certainly, just as there are exceptions to most of life's rules. But looking for the exceptions, or more importantly looking for how your current problems are the exception to this rule, will not serve you well. Solutions are found in identifying our responsibilities and acting on them, not in finding someone else at whom to point a finger.

To be clear, neither you nor your partner is responsible for Crazy being crazy or for the crazy things she does, but you are both responsible for figuring out how you enable it and how you are going to put a stop to it.

If you are prepared to accept this then you are ready to start taking back control of your life and your future. If you are not ready, if you are balking and looking for excuses, if the fear of what crazy will do is going to continue to dominate your decisions, if the fear of your partner's reaction is making you retreat, if the fear of Crazy is still greater than your need for autonomy and self-respect, then we understand.

However, it is only fair to you that you see that choice for what it is: *a decision to leave Crazy in charge of your life.* You will live with that, and with the consequences, for as long as you choose to tolerate it. At this point, it is not Crazy doing it to you. It is you doing it to yourself.

We believe that you are worth more than that, that indeed every human being is worth more than that.

Now, assuming that you have had enough of Crazy, and you are ready to take the plunge into a more functional, balanced and Crazy-less life, then there is another fundamental rule of human behavior we do well to revisit.

Behaviors tend to decrease when they cause predictable suffering for the person doing them.

We all knew this as kids, didn't we? We all remember being told that all bullies are cowards, and most of us have seen this in action at one time or another when we watched a bully, shocked and dismayed when their victim fought back, simply move on to pick on someone else who would take it.

Bullies terrorize their victims until doing so guarantees that they will suffer for doing it. Their smaller, weaker victims don't even have to be able to win the fight. All they have to do is make it painful to make them a victim. That is enough to rid most kids of a bully in their lives.

In the simplest definition, that's what Crazy is: a bully. She attacks and abuses others, including children, who can't or won't defend themselves. She uses the courts and other authorities, manipulates friends and family into doing some of her dirty work for her, but the central theme to everything she does is that those whom she abuses are not in a position fight back. Crazy banks on other people either being too polite, timid or downright scared to inflict the pain of telling her, "No."

She is the thug in the schoolyard smirking because all the teachers are on her side. She *loves* being in that position. It is her *raison d'être*. She will not give it up, ever, until it becomes so painful that she feels compelled to let go of it, until she can predict her efforts to inflict harm in your life have consequences associated with them from which she will not escape.

As we already acknowledged, there are exceptions to every rule. Alcoholics and drug addicts often continue to do the same things after experiencing severe pain and other consequences for what they do. In fact, continued use of alcohol and drugs after experiencing life consequences like job losses, legal problems and health issues is one of the ways we diagnose alcoholism and other addictions.

As a rule, though, this exception does not apply to Crazy. She is not addicted, and she is not stupid. When what she does results in her suffering—even if she makes other suffer—she finds something, or more importantly, someone else to target with her abuses. She may be nuts, but she knows what the flame on a hot stove feels like after burning her fingers a few times.

Make no mistake. She will test the resolve of anyone who has decided not to tolerate her antics. She will likely up the ante and increase the abuse the first few times she is tested in hopes that she can crush the resistance. Part of her sickness is that she views anyone not tolerating her abuse as an abuser, and for a short time it will be her mission to *win*. She likes that kind of challenge and thrives on it in the short term.

It won't last. Her payoff is to make you suffer and to do so without consequence. When it's she who suffers, that payoff is removed, and the opposite incentive is provided.

With that in mind, you and your partner must be dedicated to the idea of making her accountable for the consequences for every violation of your lives. That must hold true regardless of her initial reactions, which can include, but are not limited to, making (more) false allegations, further alienating children and the use of family courts for whatever is at her disposal to punish those who don't toe her line.

In other words, *she will do the things she has likely already been doing*, and will continue to do whether you hold your ground or not.

There is a caveat to this that is important. In some cases there are young children involved. In a small fraction of these cases there may be a potential for Crazy to react to having limits set with her by taking her anger out on the children physically, possibly even putting their safety in peril.

If you feel for any reason this is the case, then we recommend strongly that you document whatever evidence you have of that, which should be your routine with her anyway, and take it to the authorities. If you genuinely fear for the safety of your children it is your obligation to do what you have to do to protect them, but be advised we have never encountered a case where we believe that submitting to the abuses of a psychopath has protected the safety or well-being of children.

Assuming you are not concerned that children are going to be placed in imminent danger because you have decided to say goodbye to Crazy, you ready to proceed. Almost. There is one other thing that we need to make clear.

It is important for you to recognize that this is not just about you and your partner's limits and expectations with her. It is also about your expectations of him. Protecting a boundary around a relationship is the responsibility of both partners. Whether limits have to be set with Crazy, her children, your own children or all three, it is up to both partners to get the job done.

So, you not only have to decide that you are no longer surrendering your life to Crazy or the people who are acting on her behalf, you also have to decide on whether you will accept a partner who refuses to join you in stopping it. You can always make the unilateral decision to evict Crazy from your life by doing whatever you have to do to get the job done, including leaving. If he does not join you in the protection of your relationship then that may well be the only path available to you. It is a difficult decision that we urge you to take reluctantly, but the object here is to get the Crazy out of your life, to give her a pink slip and send her packing. All options should be on the table if that is to seriously be the goal.

There will be more on this in future chapters, and as the actual point of this is to give Crazy the boot while strengthening, not ending, your relationship, we are going to proceed with that in mind. Next up, a chapter about him, why he has such a hard time saying no to the nutcase and what you can do to help him find a way out of that trap.

Takeaways

- You are in charge of how you allow others to treat you.

- By not setting boundaries in relation to Crazy, you are allowing her to determine the interactions between your family and her

- These boundaries must start with your spouse—but you must first begin by helping him to see what boundaries are, why they are important, and how the entire family will benefit from them.

- We only change when our behaviors cause more pain than gain. Crazy will not change until she sees her behaviors cause her more grief than joy. Nor will your spouse change until he sees that his behaviors are allowing for more grief.

- Only you and your spouse can stop allowing Crazy to drive your family's train. This means both your spouse and Crazy have to feel the pain from their behaviors. For you, this will create some immediate pain as both your spouse and Crazy push back at the idea of change, but stay strong.

Chapter 20

Solutions: This Stuff is Hard

As you have no doubt noted through the pages of this book, we are not pulling any punches about the problems common to high-conflict, personality disordered ex-wives and girlfriends, also known as Crazy. If anything, we have been rather brutal about laying these matters out for examination. We have described their behavior, and the damage they inflict in unflinching, somewhat cold terms.

The logic in this, of course, is that sugar-coating problems may help people feel a little better about talking about them, but it does not help anyone solve anything. In fact, most of life's problems tend to get worse, depending on how much we invest in denying them. We sometimes have to ask ourselves if we want to make problems easy to talk about or if we want to fix them. Sometimes we can do both. Sometimes we can't.

With Crazy, we can't.

The problems brought on by Crazy are easy for some people to avoid dealing with precisely because they are so difficult. When children are hurt and alienated, when it is so easy for Crazy to call on courts and other authorities to express her displeasure and enforce her will, when her actions cause chaos and serious damage and when she has time and again demonstrated the willingness to go to whatever lengths are necessary to maintain her control or get her way, it can be very tempting to bury one's head in the sand. Worse yet, it becomes just as easy to sacrifice yourself with attempts to appease Crazy and steer her, hopefully, toward the creating the least possible problems for everyone.

The only problem is that in most cases, it leaves people like you finding and reading books like this, desperately looking for a way out of the mess that Crazy is making of your life.

With that in mind, we are going to tell you up front that we are going to be just as direct with you and with what you need to do, as we have been when talking about her. We are not going to help you find excuses to avoid taking the tough but necessary actions to fix this situation. We are also telling you that allowing your partner to have any excuses is a deal breaker, too. The time for looking the other way or staying quiet to keep the peace or for putting up with abuse to protect the kids, from either of you, is over.

If you are like most human beings, you will find a foot at the end of your leg. It is time for you to put it down. Nothing else will work, because nothing else can.

We are not going to tell you how to do all this in three easy steps. That sort of pipe dream is for self-help books. The hard truth is that none of this is easy, and none of it is fun. For many of you though, it is the only hope you have of regaining some control over your life and your own happiness.

We are going to call on you and your partner to make very tough choices, perhaps some of the hardest decisions you will ever make. Some of them can be gut wrenching. Some of them even harder than that.

So, before we move on to these hard solutions, that will show you how to say goodbye to Crazy, let us remind you of some basic facts that we feel you must understand and accept before the solutions we offer can be put to effective use. Always remember the following:

- **Crazy is not a rational human being with whom you can bargain.** Is this sinking in yet? Crazy does not make deals, and if she does she does not keep them. She does not respond to reason or kindness or compromise. You cannot appeal to her good judgment or her desire to do the right thing. Your willingness to compromise with Crazy will only be taken as weakness and exploited. Your insistence on trying to negotiate in good faith, and your expectation that she will somehow come around to treating you with fairness and compassion is your own form of craziness, as well as your

Achilles' heel. For you to move forward, seeing Crazy in unrealistic ways must stop.

- **Crazy is not a co-parent.** If you still have clichés like "She is still the mother of his child," floating around in your head, and you are using that to cut her some slack, then you need to go back and start this book over again. If you are going to survive this and move on, you need to quit seeing her as a co-parent and recognize her for what she really is—a woman who uses her status as the Golden Uterus to control, abuse and dominate everyone in her path. That includes the father of her children, her children, your children and you. From this point on, you and your partner must see her as the *parallel parent*, which we will discuss in *chapter 29* . From this point on, parallel parenting must be the goal. Fortunately, parallel parenting requires little to no cooperation or communication between the mother and father. If that sounds harsh, remember with whom you are dealing. Crazy doesn't cooperate. Crazy doesn't *work with*. Have you ever heard the term, "There is no "I" in team?" Well, there is no Crazy in team, either. Crazy only takes whatever rope you give her in the form of communication or concession and hangs everyone with it.

- **Crazy is not going to get better.** Are we learning this yet? Crazy is not going to read a book or visit a therapist or seclude herself in a temple in Tibet for six months and come back out a balanced and well-adjusted human being. She is not going to find religion, or join a support group of other Crazies who are trying to get better, or have a sudden spiritual awakening and suddenly quit alienating children or instigating other forms of chaos. Crazy *likes* being crazy. It is what floats her boat. The only rational and logical thing you can do is accept that and act accordingly from this point forward. You are not responsible for Crazy being crazy, but you are responsible for making decisions that reflect the fact that you are aware of it. The harsh reality is that for you to prevail in dealing with Crazy, you have to accept responsibility for making every decision necessary about cutting her out of the picture as much as possible.

- **Crazy is likely to cost you something.** If you manage to say good-bye to Crazy without it costing you anything in terms of finances, relationships or in extra life hassles, you will be very lucky. There is nothing she hates more than boundaries, or the word *no*. When you start setting those boundaries, Crazy sees this as a challenge. When you start saying no Crazy sees this as a challenge, too. Punishing people with boundaries, or who say no, has been her stock in trade her whole life. If you have been dealing with Crazy for any length of time, you already know this. But, if you are like most people, you have already entered a pattern of not saying no, of not having boundaries or of being much too hesitant to assert yourself because of the way Crazy has acted when you do. She has trained you not to say no to her. She has trained you to not have boundaries. She trains everyone in her life the same way. The time for that to have a place in your home has come to an end, and you need to be ready to dig your heels in about it and pay a price if necessary. What is it worth to you to have your life back?

- **Crazy is not human in the same sense you are.** Yes, we know that is a very extreme statement. Allow us to explain. It is not that Crazy is not really human. Of course she's human. She's not only human, but she's also likely a very sad, embittered human who is full of pain and disappointment. Unfortunately, because of the way she is, any compassion or understanding you extend is only something she will manipulate and exploit. She will bleed you of your compassion and understanding, play it for what she can get out of it and then turn on you for not having given more. You are much better off, in practical terms, to look at your family and your life as a garden and Crazy as the varmint that comes in and eats what she likes and destroys everything else that is growing. Whatever the varmint's personal story is, and no matter how much you try to placate or reason with the varmint, or even offer it something else to eat, you will always end up with a big, ransacked mess where your garden used to be. Your only solution is a sturdy, varmint-proof fence, even knowing that no fence is 100% varmint proof. Oh, and you can't buy this fence. You have to build it yourself.

- **Setting boundaries with Crazy is hard and setting boundaries with the children (when they act like Crazy) will be even harder.** We've spent a lot of time telling you what to expect when you set boundaries with Crazy. Basically, she's going to flip out and get worse. She will test the fence and push back harder just to see if she can break your fence. Be prepared for that to happen. It will most likely feel awful—like one sucker punch after the next.

Stand firm and hold your boundaries in place, because she will inevitably bring out the big guns. If she hasn't already, Crazy will drag out the next weapon and toss it at you with all her might. She's going to involve the children.

Putting up boundaries for Crazy is hard enough. When the kids are pulled into it, it's even worse.

It may come in the form of blatant disrespect for you and your spouse, for house rules, for step- or half-siblings. Your spouse may lose time with his children because the kids call asking Daddy to please cancel their visits for this or that reason. Crazy knows Dad loves his kids no matter what lies she tells the children. She will use that in order to test and break the boundaries you have put in place.

And the kids will buy into it. They will see poor Mom as the victim, poor Mom as just trying to get along and their father and you as the big meanies who tell Mom and them no. Be prepared for this. It's fence testing, and it can and will hurt. If you give in, however, you will find that things do not get better, but worse. Every time you give in to Crazy, either directly or by proxy through the kids, it increases her sense of power.

Even in this situation, having boundaries with the children and telling them no is not always a bad thing. Children need boundaries. They will push back against them, test them, rail against them and then, gradually, accept them. Don't be surprised if acceptance happens with kids long before it happens for Crazy—that is, *if* it ever happens for Crazy.

In many cases, sadly, the kids will also not accept healthy boundaries in their relationship with their father and you. If you and your husband find yourselves in this situation, you may have some incredibly difficult choices ahead, which we will discuss in *chapter 27*.

These six items are the most important points to understand before proceeding to Part Three of this book—Solutions. It is a good time to stop and review them again, asking yourself where you are with this information. Are you ready to see Crazy for who Crazy is? Are you ready to quit bargaining, compromising and placating so that you can take action to reduce Crazy's impact on your lives? Are you ready to insist that your partner stand alongside you in order to achieve this?

If you are completely sure that the answers to these questions are yes, then congratulations, you have already taken a big step toward finding solutions. If you are still hesitant, we suggest you set about identifying why and prepare to overcome your remaining obstacles in saying goodbye to Crazy.

For now let's assume you have decided to hop off the Crazy Train. Let's assume that you are completely willing to do what it takes to restore control of your life and your home, and that you are not about to let anyone get in your way.

The reality is that we have to assume that, because that kind of attitude is the only one that will work. In the pages ahead, we are going to show you how.

Takeaways

- None of this is easy.

- You will move forward as long as you keep putting one foot in front of the other. It may be slow, but it's still forward progress.

- Crazy is not going to change or be rational or co-parent or do what's best for the kids—so don't fret over that. You can only change you.

- Are you ready to change?

Part Three

Solving the Problem

We're here! We're in the home stretch! You've looked at what the problem is, and why it's hard to find good solutions. At this point, it's clear why saying goodbye to Crazy is no mean feat. It's hard. It's war.

You may have had to take a break and put this book down from time to time. This stuff can be painful and overwhelming. You and your spouse may have argued over aspects of it. That's okay. Part of being able to kiss Crazy goodbye is working through the reasons she's been allowed to behave as she has. Many of those reasons are difficult to face and change.

But you've done it, and you're at the place where, with war paint on, you are going to plan your solutions and carry them out.

Let's get to it!

Chapter 21

Putting on Your War Paint

We have spent considerable effort up to this point in the book talking about the problems you are likely experiencing. Talking about problems and sharing them with people is pretty easy, relatively speaking. At least it is for those of us who have spent countless hours having conversations with people describing the havoc and turmoil happening in their lives.

The people for whom we advocate do a great job articulating what has happened to them in meticulous detail. They can describe at great length and with disturbing clarity the events and outrages that have happened to them, often over periods spanning years.

Inevitably, when the conversation turns to discussing solutions to those problems, many of the same people who have spent hours venting about very frustrating problems in their lives become much less talkative. Some even fall silent. Frequently, this is where we see people retreat back into talking about the problem.

As one possible solution is suggested, that solution is ignored or deflected, and the conversation turns back to talking about the antics of the high-conflict ex.

A typical conversation along these lines goes something like this:

Counselor/Coach: Have you considered doing (solution A) or (solution B)?

Client: [Silence for a bit.] Did I tell you about the time she (insert one of Crazies episodes here)? Can you believe she did that?

Counselor/Coach: Yes, I can. I am really clear that she has been a destructive part of your life for a long time. The point of our discussing this is to help you find ways to discourage her from further acts like that. Now, why don't we discuss (insert solution A)?

Client: [Silence for a bit.] "Well, if I do (solution A) then she might (insert possible crazy response A). There was this one time I reacted to her in a way she didn't like, and she (insert another example of how Crazy was crazy in the past).

Counselor/Coach: Yes, we certainly know she does not have a great reaction to anyone setting limits, saying no or seeing to it that there are consequences for her actions. What we also know is that without setting limits, saying no and issuing consequences for mistreating you, it will only continue.

Client: But you don't understand. If I say no, she'll flip out. She might even (insert possible crazy response B). There was this one time she (insert possible crazy behavior C).

And the conversation goes on and on.

Here is the difficulty, folks. Your quest to evict Crazy's craziness from your life is not a negotiation. It is not the rational, fair and just discussion in which we would all like to engage in order to solve problems in our lives.

It is war. And to win it, you and your partner have to be warriors.

It means facing conflict with conviction and a refusal to retreat. It means making a decision, and a pact with each other that, come hell or high water, you are going to stay the course and bring sanity back into your lives, even if there is a cost associated with it.

It means staying focused on the solutions, not the problems.

If you are only willing to say goodbye to Crazy when it means doing so without her becoming upset or reacting poorly, then you have already lost. You can trust in the fact that she has known this a lot longer than you have.

One of Crazy's greatest skills is in assessing your tolerance for pain and limits for conflict and knowing exactly how much pressure she has to exert in order to get you to "cry uncle." It is likely that she has done this innumerable times in the past.

Please don't misunderstand. We are not trying to make Crazy a different person. That is a hopeless quest. The person who has to change is you. Where you have tolerated Crazy in the past has to become just that—the past. Where you have given in after saying no also has to become a thing of the past.

By this point in the book, we hope that both you and your partner are reading it because you will need each other to make this work. You will have to be a unified team with one, singular objective. *Crazy's control over your lives has to go.* It is not up for discussion or compromise. It is as certain as the fact that you both need food to eat and air to breath.

Anything less will produce failure.

This starts by embracing a discussion of the solutions. The time for obsessing over what Crazy has done to you in the past or might do in the future has come to an end.

We do not suggest that you ignore the likelihood of her potential actions. Predicting her retaliation and being prepared to weather it, as well as turn it into another consequence for her, is an essential part of your winning strategy.

You must be willing to pay for your freedom. You may have to accept that Crazy will badmouth and demonize you to the children for as long as they will listen. It may mean that she will do everything she can to increase child support and to use the courts to further disrupt your lives. No one can guarantee that she can be stopped from doing this. We can only assure you that if you are not willing to make her pay a price for her misdeeds, then you have far less of a chance that she will quit committing them.

What price are you willing to pay to have your lives and your dignity restored? What are you willing to endure to regain ownership of your day-to-day existence? Crazy is not going to give you those things. If you want them, you have to take them. And if you are going to take them, you must know in advance how you plan to do it.

The hypothetical conversation between counselor and client earlier in this chapter is an example of how to keep Crazy in your lives. It is a prescription for failure.

The time has come to quit talking about how crazy Crazy is. We know how crazy she is, and we know that she will be crazier before this is over. That is the path you are choosing, and we want to help you walk it. But first, you must put on your war paint.

Takeaways

- Talking about the problem is easy. Talking about the solutions is hard.

- In order to say goodbye to Crazy, you must see this not as a negotiation, but as war.

- Crazy will be as destructive as possible—but how is that any different? She will do that anyway.

- You are in a war to take back your home and life. It's war to change yourself—not Crazy. Crazy isn't going to change a thing.

- You know Crazy will retaliate. Plan for that. Be prepared for it. It's no different than what she already does. The difference is you will make your life better.

Chapter 22

The Contract Crazy Doesn't Get to Sign, But You Do!

Actually, both you and your partner get to sign this contract.

We have written this book with two different audiences in mind. The first audience is you, the wives and girlfriends of men once married to Crazy. The second audience is your partner. We hope that you will read this together. We have focused on you as a couple for one simple reason.

If you cannot form a unified team to solve this problem together, then your chances for success have likely already been dashed.

Crazy cannot be exiled by a divided or broken team. Like a lone person on a teeter-totter, it is a nonstarter. It will take both of you to maintain a healthy boundary around your relationship against Crazy.

The only boundary that you alone can control is the one around you, even if that means defending a boundary you must have with your partner. If he is the chink in the armor protecting your relationship, that will have to change. Otherwise, you will be faced with the possibility that the only way to say goodbye to Crazy is to say it to him first.

Ending your marriage is not the goal here. Indeed the goal is just the opposite. The goal is to enhance your relationship through teamwork and unity, the things that build trust and intimacy. We wrote this book with the hopes of that very thing happening, but we are aware that this book isn't a substitute for an active, committed and strong partnership.

Crazy is an expert at manipulating and controlling people. She will hone in on your husband's weaknesses and use him like an errand boy to undermine your efforts. She will do it with ease, and there will be nothing you can do to stop her. She will target your weaknesses, as well.

This brings us to one of the must haves, which is the full participation of both of you as a team dedicated to the same goals. This is the time for both of you to stop and assess, because this is the moment that will define your relationship and Crazy's influence in it, now and into the future. Are you both on the same page and ready to change?

In a perfect world that means your partner has already started reading this book and is on board with the program. The contract below, either at signing time or shortly thereafter, will inform you with 100 % clarity where you both stand, and what you are both willing to do.

There will be plenty of times in the future when you will laugh about the days you used to live under Crazy's spell, but this is a moment to embrace some grim realism. If either one of you cannot be relied upon to honor the contract, then the contract means nothing. We suggest that you view signing it as a turning point in your lives, something to be done circumspectly by both parties. It is an agreement that is as important as your marriage, and on which your marriage likely hinges more than your original vows.

In fact, if you read it correctly, you will see it is what marriage vows are supposed to be—complete and total commitment to putting the relationship first. If either of you cannot sign, you're unlikely to succeed in saying goodbye to Crazy.

A Contract for Sanity

We, the undersigned, are now faced with the serious problem of individual(s), herein after referred to as Crazy, who are having a negative impact on our relationship and our family. We have decided together, freely and willingly, to combine our efforts as a team to end the effect of Crazy, as much as humanly possible.

We recognize and acknowledge that efforts to find reasonable solutions or compromises with Crazy come at very high cost and very low yield. We understand that solutions for us are to be found **only** with our unilateral action for self-preservation—forsaking any hope that Crazy can be bargained with or changed.

We pledge to follow through with the life changes required to face and, as much as possible, remove Crazy from our daily routine and our consciousness.

Signed _____ Signed _____

Chapter 23

Identifying and Using Crazy's Fears to Protect Yourself

Does the title of this chapter seem Machiavellian? Does reading it make you cringe a little or a lot? That's understandable. It probably not only seems harsh, but cold and calculating, too. Exploiting someone's fears sounds like something, well, like something Crazy would do. And she does, regularly and without giving it a second thought.

There's a difference, though.

The purpose of identifying and leveraging Crazy's fears is not to maliciously torture her for sport or vengeance. It is so you can protect yourselves within the bounds of the law and be better able to deliver natural consequences when Crazy inevitably tries to blitzkrieg your boundaries. To say goodbye to Crazy, you must make it too painful or too boring for her to continue to mess with you. Why?

Because nothing else works.

Obviously, this is not something we recommend doing with rational and reasonable people who respect boundaries and obey laws. Crazy is neither rational nor reasonable, and she sees any boundary you put in place as a call to arms.

The Five Fears

As mentioned in Part One, Crazy is typically driven by five fundamental fears, which are:

- The fear of abandonment.
- The fear of loss of control.
- The fear of feeling or appearing inferior or inadequate.
- The fear of loss of resources.
- The fear of exposure.

Crazy may fear all of these things equally, and some more than others. Her biggest fear(s) may change periodically depending on what's happening in her life at any given moment. Your objective is to identify and understand which of these fears motivate your Crazy and to learn how and when to leverage them effectively.

The fear of abandonment. This is a big fear for many a Crazy—and many a codependent. We've said it before, and we'll say it again: you cannot abandon an adult. You *leave* an adult. Actions have consequences. A natural consequence for abusing the person you claim to love is that, eventually, the loved one may decide he or she has had enough and *leave* you.

Even if Crazy is the one who initiated the divorce, she still may perceive it as an abandonment by her ex—especially if her ex eventually recouples, with you for instance. Even if Crazy and your husband were divorced long before you met him, in her mind she believes he abandoned her for you. Crazy often expects her ex(es) to forever remain on standby should she need something from them—attention, love, money, to triangulate with a current target, an on-demand babysitter or just the security that someone is available. Meanwhile, she can date and remarry as often as she likes.

Crazy probably has reasons going back to childhood that cause her pathological fear of abandonment, but we're not here to figure that out. What you and your husband need to figure out is how to make this fear work for you. We presume your goal is to eliminate Crazy from your lives as much as you possibly can. Crazy will most likely experience it as an abandonment, which she will fight against. If there aren't any shared minor children this is a non-issue. You end any and all contact. Yesterday.

If there are shared minor children, you can try using Crazy's fear of abandonment as a consequence. For example, Crazy sometimes likes to send angry and accusatory emails and texts that have nothing to do with the children or parenting. The consequence is that you do not respond to those messages. You only respond when Crazy sends relevant and civil messages. We are aware that may never happen, but we are pretty certain it won't happen as long as you are willing to respond to messages that are neither relevant nor civil.

Urban legend has it that police can prevent a lot of crime by paying attention to the small stuff. The thinking is that if police are visibly going after the pettiest of crimes it prevents larger crimes from happening. That is the kind of cop you want to be in the jurisdiction of your new life.

Be prepared to immediately terminate any communication you have with her in which she is not conducting herself as though she is sane and reasonable. Never forget that she has more than sufficient capability for reason and fairness when she knows she has no other option, but seldom before that happens. Case in point—many Crazies can get up and go to a job every day, follow the rules, treat people civilly and rationally and even excel professionally. Sure, some Crazies go to work and stir up as much crap as possible, but even those are usually cautious enough to know which lines not to cross. They are fully conscious of their actions and in complete control of their behavior when they know they have to be.

The critical factor here is that you are sending Crazy the message that she has one way and one way only to communicate with you. We suggest that this be the general approach, even if your contact with Crazy is rare. Remember, even if we don't get all the way there, we are aiming for 0% crazy.

The fear of loss of control. Divorce and shared custody are a huge loss of control for Crazy. Shared children are an efficient way for Crazy to continue to have some form of control over your husband and you. Crazy will try to control access. She will try to control how your husband parents the children and your interaction with them.

She may be texting or calling the kids non-stop while they are with you to maintain her sense of control.

We strongly encourage you to allow Crazy NO control over your lives. Let parallel parenting kick in. Straightforwardly address any problems that this may have caused between you and your children. Don't be afraid to tell them the truth. All of it. Parent according to your values and explain the reasons for doing so to your children. You don't have to demonize their mother to tell them your side of the story. Simply explaining that you, like anyone else, insist upon having your own rules in your own home. This concept is sensible enough to register with most kids. So will similar explanations for other problems between you and Crazy, especially when delivered by a loving father.

Your kids may not grasp all of it at the time, but those are some valuable seeds to plant. You never know when a young person will reevaluate their lives.

Oh, and one last item. While we suggest direct and honest explanations for your shared children, we don't consider telling them, "Because I am the parent and I say so," to be child abuse when they refuse to listen. When children won't accept rational explanations, laying down the law is in order. It is called parenting. They will likely only get from you.

Remember, your house—your rules. Not Crazy's. Anything else is the kind of control Crazy never should have had in the first place.

The fear of feeling or appearing inferior or inadequate. Rejection, whether real or imagined, is a trigger for Crazy that makes her feel inferior. Most non-disordered people feel this way after being rejected, but only temporarily. Where Crazy differs from most people is that she is likely to become highly destructive to herself and others when she feels rejected and "less than."

Crazy's feelings of rejection and inferiority are amplified exponentially when her ex recouples. Not only are these feelings amplified, Crazy may very well go into a full-blown narcissistic rage. Crazy often sees the new partner of her ex as competition, even when Crazy herself is remarried. It doesn't matter if she has a new enabler/target/accomplice, she still expects to come first—with your husband, the kids and even her former in-laws.

This a common precursor to child alienation efforts from Crazy. In her mind if you do not continue to put her first after parting ways, she experiences it as a grave wound and insult. She will chronically share her feelings about this with the children, likely before she drags other adults into the matter.

To put it more succinctly, Crazy is programmed to set up tests that you can't help but fail, then lose her marbles when you do. She is driven to obsessively create the very rejection she fears the most, resulting in the humiliation and feelings of inferiority of which she is so terrified. Her self-fulfilling prophesy spirals causing her to react histrionically. Chaos ensues, often damaging everyone in her proximity.

The fear of loss of resources. Crazy has a currency, and she will wage all-out war to keep it. Money. Attention. Social status. Power. Material goods. Public image. We know of cases in which Crazy, well, there's no way to pretty this up, has sold the children to their father for money in the divorce settlement. There are also cases in which Crazy dragged out the divorce as long as she could because she didn't want to cease being *Mrs. Somebody*, even though she would openly talk about how much she despised her husband.

If you can figure out Crazy's currency, you might be able to bribe her with it if she gives up something you want, like more time with the kids. For example, Crazy Martha Stewart Wannabe loves throwing elaborate birthday parties "for the kids." She makes origami Transformers table settings, organic, gluten-free *everything*, decorations, face painting, personalized cupcakes for every child, games and a bouncy house because, hey, why not set a 5-year old's expectations ever-increasingly high? Anything she can think of to show her guests that she's Mother of the Year, she does it. She likes being the most amazing hostess ever.

How do you leverage this?

Have your attorney forward a proposed motion to her attorney (or to Crazy directly if she's been fired from yet another attorney) requesting a motion to amend the court order to include alternating who throws the children's birthday parties first. When she pushes back, have your attorney explain that throwing birthday parties for your kids is important to you, as well. You also want your kids to have those very special memories of your parties. Tell her you want to throw the first birthday party so your child remembers you first for their odd numbered birthdays. (Yes, Crazy can get this crazy).

Meanwhile, you couldn't care less if she wants to throw children's birthday parties like she's a Kardashian sister. Offer to concede birthday party priority to her *if* she gives you something in return, like final decision making for the kids' education.

Please keep in mind that these are not matters you settle by negotiating or discussing directly with Crazy or your children. They are offers you should forward to her legal counsel through your legal counsel and no one else. Also, remember that the agreement will mean nothing at all until it is recognized by the court.

If Crazy does not have counsel, let your lawyer talk to her directly. Following through with these steps ensures that you maintain your pledge to avoid any and all unnecessary contact with Crazy, giving her less opportunity to throw a wrench into the works.

The fear of exposure. Some Crazies are out there loud and proud. They see nothing wrong at all with their behavior, and they don't care who knows it. We think they are the minority. Crazy will most often go to extremes to make sure that what happens behind closed doors never comes to light. Crazy will launch preemptory smear campaigns. She will make false allegations of abuse or other criminal activity, threaten to keep the children from you—whatever it takes.

If you have meticulously documented evidence of her misdeeds, such as criminal activity, substance abuse, physical and emotional abuse of you and the children, infidelities, etc., and she doesn't want it to come out in open court, this could give you leverage to get a more equitable custody or financial arrangement.

We are absolutely not suggesting you blackmail Crazy. That would be illegal and unethical. However, if any of the information you have is relevant to the well being of the children, such as substance abuse, criminal behavior, physical and emotional violence, child endangerment or exposing the children to lewd behavior, it is fair game and should be brought to the attention of the court. Period.

If the information you have isn't necessarily damaging to the children, but could be personally embarrassing for Crazy, it may also be fair game. Infidelity isn't supposed to matter in no-fault states, but it can and does come out in divorce trials. If Crazy cares about her public image, she will not want her affair(s) exposed—especially if she portrays herself as some holier-than-thou Mother of the Year.

If you're going to use public exposure as leverage *do it through your attorney*. Your attorney should convey to Crazy's attorney that the information she doesn't want to expose will be exposed in a public hearing if she won't come to a reasonable agreement on the issues. Use this fear judiciously, legally and only if you are absolutely prepared to carry it out if Crazy calls your bluff. This applies to leveraging all her fears, actually, but to this one most of all.

Takeaways

- Crazy is driven by five fears.

- Identifying and understanding these fears can help you protect yourself from Crazy by tailoring consequences for her boundary violations.

- If you go down this route, we recommend you do so with the help of an attorney and always stay within the bounds of the law.

Chapter 24

Safety First: Assessing the Threat Crazy Poses and Your Vulnerabilities

In previous chapters, we explained why saying goodbye to Crazy is so damned difficult. Not only can saying goodbye to Crazy be difficult, there are often personal safety issues involved, too.

Essentially, we are talking about wresting control of your lives away from someone with sociopathic traits who likes to be in charge and force compliance through fear, guilt, shame and obligation. *These are potentially dangerous personalities.* It is vital that you do not underestimate her capacity to do harm or naively misattribute a sense of decency to Crazy. These are two of the biggest mistakes non-sociopathic people make when dealing with sociopaths.

Even worse, since Crazy was once intimately involved with your partner, she poses the ultimate "insider threat." She probably knows his fears, weaknesses, regrets and sore spots all too well. She knows how to obtain compliance from your husband and has been able do so based solely upon the fear of what she *might* do or is *capable* of doing without ever having to lift a finger.

Fear of retaliation is one of the biggest obstacles many people face in saying goodbye to Crazy. Saying no to crazy, ignoring her antics, going low/no contact, refusing to play her psychotic reindeer games and implementing and maintaining boundaries will undoubtedly—at least temporarily—escalate the worst of Crazy's behaviors and abuses. Before you and your partner begin to implement the strategies outlined in this book, we recommend you determine exactly how much of a threat Crazy poses to you and your loved ones.

Crazy's level of threat is determined by her capability and intent to do harm. Capability is what she *can* do. Intent is what she *wants* to do. If Crazy can't or doesn't want to do anything, then she poses little or no threat. For example, she may want to get your husband fired (intent), but your husband's boss knows she is a whack job and is disinclined to believe her lies (zero capability).

Alternately, your husband's boss might believe Crazy's lies, but if your husband loses his job, it means a possible reduction in spousal and child support monies and Crazy doesn't want that (zero intent).

There may be other variables that diminish the threat Crazy poses. For example, has she recoupled? Is she busy trying to trap a new target? Does she have a new money source to exploit? Is she divorcing her most recent spouse and not have enough bandwidth to harass you? Does she have a job or other time obligations?

Anything that decreases Crazy's capability and intent to do harm is useful information to have in assessing how much of a threat she is at any given time. For instance, if Crazy is in the throes of her third divorce, strategically it would be a good time for your husband to take her to court for a custody change or any other issues that need addressing. It's difficult to fight two legal battles simultaneously, even for Crazy.

The other variables you need to consider in risk assessment are your vulnerabilities to Crazy, which are unique to you and your husband. What are your Achilles' heels? Is your husband still in denial about the true nature of his ex? Does Crazy have sensitive information about you or your husband that you don't want made public? Is your husband still seeking Crazy's approval? Is he susceptible to guilt trips? Is he afraid of Crazy? Does he still believe Crazy can be reasoned with? Does he believe he deserves Crazy's abuse? Does he believe appeasing Crazy is an effective strategy? Is he afraid Crazy will turn the kids against him? Is he conflict avoidant? Do you have resources to defend yourselves in court if Crazy makes false allegations? Do you find it hard not to bite on Crazy's bait?

Failure to identify and eliminate your vulnerabilities increases Crazy's ability to do harm. Good news—your vulnerabilities are under your control. You may or may not be able to reduce all of your vulnerabilities in the short term, but you can over time.

One of the most effective ways to reduce your vulnerabilities is to have strong boundaries. Insiders have something that outsiders don't—access. To control access, you have to have *boundaries*. Crazy typically doesn't respect boundaries, and you may not effectively set and enforce them. Whether the boundaries are physical or emotional, they serve the same purpose. They keep Crazy *out*.

There are certain factors and triggers that increase the likelihood that Crazy will escalate emotional, financial, psychological and/or physical violence. You probably already know what many of them are. Common ones include being held accountable, being denied money or other resources, being told no, having boundaries, limits or restrictions placed upon her, being truthful with your children, her ex recoupling, holidays, dates or anniversaries that carry some special meaning for Crazy, having abandonment issues triggered, feeling out of control, etc.

Perhaps the most important variable to consider in assessing the risk Crazy poses is does she eventually respond to boundaries and consequences, even if it takes her a few weeks, months or years? Or is she the kind of Crazy who doesn't care about consequences, no matter how painful they are for her?

The second kind of Crazy is likely to be the most dangerous and possibly deadly. They are the familial version of suicide bombers. They are family terrorists who, even if they have something to lose, will continue to escalate, violate court orders and break laws, sometimes to the point of lethality.

If you are dealing with this kind of Crazy, the sanest, healthiest choice you can make may be to drop the rope and walk away, *unless* there are other variables working in your favor. For example, the family court system understands how crazy Crazy is and works with you to protect yourself and your family. The same goes for law enforcement and any mental health professionals involved in your case.

One couple we know figured out their vulnerabilities and the threat their Crazy posed by sitting down and making a list. One column listed all the actions they could take—legal, financial and behavioral.

The middle column listed all the things Crazy could do in retaliation for each of the actions they could take—what they felt her most likely reaction would be. They based this on their knowledge of how she reacted in the past.

In the third column, they listed how they, as a couple and as individuals, would respond to whatever crazy reaction Crazy had. What they found was that they were indeed able to face Crazy head on. They realized it wouldn't always be easy. In some cases, it could be downright hurtful. Particularly where the man's children were involved. However, that list with three columns was a life changer for them.

Prior to making that list together, there was a great deal of fear and conjecture. What would Crazy do if they did this or that? Fear is a powerful emotion, as we have shown. Looking at the fear and accepting the potentially negative outcome and knowing they could manage it took away a great deal of the fear.

Don't be afraid to look at the fear head on. Only then can you plan how to handle anything crazy that Crazy does and, if necessary, involve the appropriate law enforcement or legal professionals.

Crazy is crazy. This means she will hurt others, even children, to get what she wants. You must accept this fact, painful though it is, even if Crazy is the mother of children you love. She's crazy. That means even children are not safe.

As the sane adults, it's your job to make things safer. No one can ever be truly safe with Crazy, but you can make it more so.

Takeaways

- Crazy will hurt anyone who gets in her way. This means the children are at risk, as well. You have to accept this.

- There is risk involved for everyone when you say goodbye to Crazy. It doesn't mean you should not say goodbye, but you need to face and accept the risk.

- Crazy will use her insider knowledge to make any plans you have to change painful to you and your spouse.

- You and your spouse need to look at all the risks, and any actual threats Crazy poses. Plan for her negative reactions. Decide before you start the process how you want to address her reactions before they happen. This will make them easier to handle as you are dealing with them.

- Look for ways to minimize contact. Less contact is better when any contact is generally going to be negative.

- Work as a team. This will not get better if the two of you do not work together.

- Be honest! If you are scared of something that doesn't scare your spouse, say so. See #6 above.

Chapter 25

Crazy-Proofing and Crazy-Busting

Most people have heard of "baby-proofing" a home to make it safe for newborns and toddlers. Crazy-proofing is similar. Crazy-proofing is the boundaries you and your partner put in place to protect yourselves from Crazy and her shenanigans. Crazy-busting is what you do when you enforce these boundaries and deliver consequences.

The following list of Crazy-proofing and Crazy-busting tactics is not exhaustive. These are some of the most basic, best practices we have discovered in our work with others and in our own lives that help to keep Crazy a healthy distance away. Like Timbuktu, for instance. We go over the most important strategies individually in the chapters that follow.

- **Do not negotiate with terrorists (or Crazy—same difference).** Crazy is a black-and-white/all-or-nothing thinker. In Crazy's mind, all interactions are a zero-sum game. In order for Crazy to feel she is winning, you and your husband must lose, and lose spectacularly. There is no negotiating and compromising with Crazy, because the only way Crazy typically gives an inch is if a judge makes her do it or if she is seeking social recognition for being "such a good person." Remember, Crazy only gives something to get something. Remember this, and use it to your advantage whenever possible.

- **You did not break Crazy and you cannot fix or save Crazy.** You cannot love Crazy well. Being kind and friendly to Crazy makes you vulnerable. Even feeling sorry for Crazy is dangerous. Feeling sympathy for Crazy is a slippery slope that may lead to enabling Crazy. Wait until the children age out before you allow yourselves to feel sorry for her and then feel sorry for her from a safe distance once she can no longer harm you.

- **Accept that you might not be able to save the children from their mother, especially if they choose to align themselves with her.** You will be vilified by Crazy no matter how much you appease her, allow her to steamroll your boundaries and extort money and other resources from you. She will do her best to hurt you, and if she has to hurt the children in the process, she will not hesitate to do so. You and your partner are the only grown-ups in this situation. Crazy "wins" by placing you in no-win situations. Since you're going to portrayed as the bad guys no matter what you do, do what is best for you and the children. Even if that means telling the children no and setting appropriate boundaries if they become foot soldiers for Crazy. Your goal should be to teach your children right from wrong, provide them a safe, structured, consistent, loving respite from Crazy, and show them alternatives to what Crazy teaches them and hope it sticks.

- **No more making excuses for Crazy.** Some men have difficulty fully admitting that they made a gross error in judgment in marrying and breeding with Crazy. Periodically, you will hear them say things like, "She's not that bad" or "But she's a good mother." Husband, boyfriend or fiancé, if you are reading this, *yes, Crazy really is that bad and she is NOT a good mother*. Good mothers do not use their children as weapons. Good mothers do not teach their children to hate and fear their fathers. Good mothers do not use their children to extort money and other resources from you. Good mothers do not put their own self-interests and petty nonsense ahead of their children, so quit lying to yourself and stop making excuses for her and minimizing her abominable behavior. All that does is make it easier for Crazy to manipulate you.

- **BOUNDARIES.** Crazy hates boundaries. She typically experiences boundaries as "controlling." In reality, they obstruct her from being able to torment, harass and abuse you. Similarly, Crazy experiences being held accountable and consequences for her behavior as "abusive." It's quite a system Crazy has worked out for herself. You'll know how good your boundaries are by the decibel level of squealing with which Crazy responds.

- **Go no contact or, if that is not possible because there are shared children, go low contact.** If at all possible, keep all communication in writing and make it brief. This serves several purposes. One, you have a record of her asshattery (if she's arrogant or stupid enough to put her asshattery in writing). Two, it is much easier to detect the manipulations, distortions, contradictions and other gyrations in writing.

- **Emotionally detach and disengage.** Crazy is a button-pusher. If you have a button, Crazy will find it and press it like a starving rat desperate for its next yum-yum pellet. You must learn to emotionally detach from Crazy's antics. If Crazy wants nothing else, she wants your attention. Good attention, bad attention—it's all the same to Crazy. Losing your patience, losing your temper or engaging in any emotionally charged way rewards Crazy, so you need to starve the beast. If you combine this rule with no or low contact and robust boundaries, you will be well on your way to saying goodbye to Crazy.

- **No good deed goes unpunished.** If you share children, this is why you do not deviate from the Court Order. Ever. No changing custody days. No special favors or exemptions. Crazy does not reciprocate kindness and will view any deviations from the Court Order as a green light to demolish your boundaries. Give Crazy an inch, and she'll make a grab for your kidneys.

- **When it comes to Crazy, it is better to be the smart guy than the nice guy.** Check your chivalry and nice girl or nice guy-ness at the door. It will get you nowhere with Crazy except squarely under her boot heel. We are not suggesting that you be cruel or hostile. Developing an emotionally detached, no nonsense and business-like demeanor with Crazy when you must interact with her will serve you far better.

- **Stop saying, "How high?" when Crazy says, "JUMP!"** Learn to distinguish between communications from Crazy that require an immediate response, a delayed response, or no response. If you are practicing low contact with Crazy, the only communications that require a reply are ones in which the children are having a medical emergency or if there is a family emergency, like a death in the family. First, you will need to train Crazy to ONLY contact you in writing. Responding to neither her voicemails nor calling her should eventually accomplish this.

- **You cannot co-parent with Crazy. You parent around Crazy or *parallel parent*.** Co-parenting requires that both parents be able to compromise, share control, set aside any petty differences and lingering animosity and *parent*. If Crazy was not capable of these things while still married, she is less capable of them after divorce. Parallel parenting is a sanity preserver and one of the most effective ways to say goodbye to Crazy when children are involved.

- **Do not "date" Crazy.** Your partner should not have one-on-one meetings with Crazy—even if it is under the guise of "family therapy" unless you are court ordered to do so. Weaseling solo face time with your partner feeds into Crazy's fantasy that she is still the number one priority in your husband's life, and that they will always have a *special connection*.

- **Do not allow Crazy to manipulate you through intermediaries—including friends, family *and the children*.** Once Crazy figures out that you're serious about enforcing boundaries, she is likely to pull out the big guns. This includes trying to manipulate and control you through any mutual friends, her family, your partner's family, co-workers, employers, pastors, Crazy-enabling therapists, attorneys, law enforcement, judges and, of course, the children.

- **Don't let Crazy in the door.** This one is simple, efficient and can prevent a lot of problems. Always, always exchange the kids at a neutral location like school, the parking lot of a fast food restaurant, or even a police station. If you can think of a good reason for Crazy to be allowed into your home or for you to enter her home, we can tell you why you are going to fail. Keeping Crazy from passing through the threshold of your home is a basic tenet of saying goodbye to Crazy. Crazy should have a clear understanding that for her your home is off-limits.

- **Only go dumpster diving when you are collecting evidence for court or therapeutic evaluations.** Some people with a Crazy in their lives are attracted to Crazy's social media like a moth to a flame. There are good reasons for keeping tabs on Crazy's social media, and there are unhealthy reasons for doing so. Healthy reasons include gathering documentation for court. We never cease to be amazed by the over-sharing some Crazies do on Facebook and similar platforms. There are cases in which fathers have won custody based on Crazy's Facebook posts and tweets. On the other hand, stalking her Facebook page, when you do not have a legitimate reason to do so, such as pending legal action, just gives Crazy real estate in your head, and we strongly advise against that.

Now that we've looked at some basic Crazy-proofing and Crazy-busting techniques, we're going to explore them in greater detail in the chapters that follow. You may find this too much to digest and remember all at once. That's okay. Set the book down and return and refer to it as needed.

Takeaways

- You must Crazy-proof your life from Crazy.

- You didn't break Crazy, therefore, you cannot fix her. Nor are you obligated to even try to fix her.

- You may not be able to save any children from the Crazy that is their mom. She IS Crazy, so having Crazy as a mom is something the kids will have to learn to live with.

- Don't make excuses for Crazy. She's a grown woman. She owns her choices.

- Boundaries are your friends. Don't be afraid of them, even when they are hard.

- Be smart, not nice. Crazy will never reciprocate any acts of kindness from you.

Chapter 26

Boundaries:
Why We Don't Negotiate with
Emotional Terrorists

During the 80s and 90s, *boundaries* was one of the most commonly used and least understood terms in the mental health field. We talked endlessly with people about having boundaries, about what we should do and how we should react when those boundaries were violated by others. It was a part of the psychobabble jargon of the time, and as such, its meaning and value were often lost in the effort to sound trendy.

But psychobabble aside, boundaries are an incredibly important thing to understand. In fact, this entire book is meaningless without a good working knowledge of what boundaries are and what they mean to a healthy, functional manner of living.

So let's take a moment to address the basics here.

Boundaries are self-constructed walls of protection around your personal security, self-respect and your *identity as a person*. They are the arbiter of whom you let in to your life, how often and how far, and what you will tolerate and what you won't. They let you know when to say yes or no to anything another human being asks of you, and when properly maintained, they give you the strength to say yes or no with conviction and authority.

They are a border you have around yourself, your relationships, your children, your home and your peace of mind.

This is critical to healthy living because boundaries are literally all you have to keep other people from taking advantage of you. And, importantly, having good boundaries means you will tend to attract people who won't try to take advantage of you in the first place: people with healthy boundaries of their own.

For instance, if you have ever had a friend who would not carry their financial weight, or who constantly hit you up for loans, your boundaries determined how annoying and prolonged that situation became.

People who find it difficult to say no when they want to, or who cave in with enough pressure or guilt, are the same ones who will be dealing with that leech for a long time, often deeply resentful of it. It might cost them a great deal of money and frustration before they can summon the will to put a stop to it.

Most of us have been though this at one time or another or we know someone who has. Without fail, the only answer to the problem was to say no and mean it. In other words, for the individual to protect their own security and peace of mind, they had to form a boundary and refuse to compromise it.

This should be ringing some bells for anyone who found it necessary to read this book.

As we have discussed at some length already, Crazy is often someone who is either personality disordered or who has those traits. What you and your partner have experienced from her is a chronic and pervasive disrespect for your personal boundaries. That includes the boundaries around your relationship, your home, your peace of mind, your financial security and even your children.

Almost every aspect of your life is something that she has invaded, time after time. There likely appears no end in sight. *There will not be unless you and your partner put an end to it.*

This is where we come to a point of information that is crucial for you to understand. It is important to know that boundaries represent something very different to Crazy than the rest of the population.

Crazy is not clueless. In fact, she has much more acumen for human boundaries than the average person ever will in a lifetime. *This is because Crazy, in all her forms, is an emotional predator whose modus operandi is to analyze the boundaries of others, size up their weaknesses and strengths, and then set out to destroy those boundaries in order to gain control and administer abuse.*

Please stop and consider that for a moment. As a matter of fact, consider it for quite a while. The importance of understanding that basic fact about the Crazy in your life cannot be overstated.

With most of us, we find out where we can and cannot go with other people because they let us know where their boundaries are. Take our friend the leech for a moment. They are attracted to people who feel guilty for not helping (poor boundaries with their money), but for the most part when they run into a wall with someone, they will just move on to someone less defended.

Crazy has a very different reaction. She views any and all boundaries as threats to her ability to control and abuse people at will. To Crazy, a stop sign actually reads "ATTACK!"

And that is precisely what she does.

She did in her relationship with your partner, and it continues to this day, only now it involves you and your children, if you have them. She considers every boundary you have, and the ones you try to construct around your relationship, as something she *must* destroy. Taking measure of how much she has affected your home life will let you know how well she is doing.

It is likely that when you look back on all the damage she has rained down on your family life, all of it was from attacks on your boundaries, or because there is a well-worn footpath where you did not have them. She has thrown everything into it, including courtrooms, children and finances. She has manipulated and sabotaged visitation to attack your peace of mind and any predictability in which you might take comfort. She has used the children's lack of developed boundaries and played their emotions to poison their minds with toxic messages about you and about their father.

She is an expert at this stuff, and a deadly one at that.

There is no getting around it. If there is a test of your relationship, it is not *her*; it is you and your partner's ability to establish boundaries and to trust each other to stand up for them. The moment you begin to compromise those boundaries, even a little, you lose.

Your relationship loses. Your children lose. Your family loses.

Our friend the leech was only a problem as long as it was difficult to say no and stick to it. Once that changed, it stopped the bleeding. Note that the leech did not change a bit. He or she is still a leech, but has been forced to seek enabling elsewhere.

And of course, when you are dealing with children and a high-conflict ex like Crazy, the stakes are higher and things are more complicated. But you still have to approach it with the same knowledge.

Get it once and for all; Crazy is not going to change. Ever.

Change begins with a mutual, clear and trustworthy agreement on where the boundaries are around your relationship and your family, and the knowledge that those boundaries are only going to be worth the résolve you both put in to them.

That may well mean that the first place for you to begin is with your boundaries with *him*. If your boundaries are not sufficient to demand that he protects your relationship, then you must start by addressing that first.

Very often the children of "second" families and children from the first family are involved in the dysfunction created by the ex. Many of them are alienated, having their minds poisoned against the father, against his new partner, or both.

While we never forget that these children are victims of this emotional predator as much as anyone else, it is also critical to not only have boundaries to protect them, but boundaries *with* them as well.

Frequently, the children of this kind of broken family behave caustically with Dad's new partner, or with Dad himself. Children from one family may be hostile to children from the other family. All of this goes back to the emotional toxicity that Crazy has injected into everyone's family life.

If you want to say goodbye to Crazy, you must be prepared to do it whether it is coming directly from Crazy herself, or by proxy from the children or anyone else connected to your family.

By tolerating destructive and abusive treatment from children, which they are conducting on behalf of a retributive, vindictive mother, you are not only allowing Crazy to run your show, you are colluding with her on the psychological abuse of your children.

Make no mistake about it. Sabotaging the relationship between a parent and a child is severe emotional abuse and can lead to scores of debilitating problems that can last the span of your children's lives. If you tolerate it, you are surrendering them to the abuse.

This is a regular occurrence in many families who are being attacked by a high conflict ex. It is frequently, unwittingly enabled by fathers and their new partners. While you may not be able to stop the abuse completely, you can quit enabling it.

New partners may feel hesitant to have firm boundaries with those children, either out of a desire to avoid conflict or because they feel out of place in a disciplinary role with their partner's children.

Fathers often balk at setting needed limits because they feel guilty for what the divorce or breakup has already done to the children, or because they have always had poor boundaries, which helped them get into this mess to begin with.

Either way, there is no way out without two adults committed to a zero tolerance policy for anyone, including their own children, to abuse their relationship or either partner in it, which we discuss in the following chapter in more detail.

Suffice it to say for now that what we want to get across here is that any possible solution to what you have experienced is inextricably tied to both halves of your partnership drawing a line in the sand, and supporting each other 100%, at *all* times, for defending those lines.

Takeaways

- Boundaries are critical to all aspects of healthy living—not just in dealing with Crazy.

- The only boundaries Crazy allows and respects are her own. No one else is allowed to have them, and should others have them, Crazy sees that as a sign to attack. Because no one other than Crazy is allowed boundaries.

- This is a test of your relationship—the ability of you and your partner to establish and uphold boundaries in relation to Crazy. Regardless of whether the attack on them comes from Crazy herself or from the children by proxy, only you and your spouse can enforce your boundaries.

- If you do not establish and uphold boundaries for your marriage and your family, you will lose any chance of peace and harmony in both.

Chapter 27

Setting Boundaries with Alienated Children

If it hasn't become clear yet, Crazy can cause a lot of damage. Her most brutal handiwork, however, is that involving the children. Because Crazy can and does abuse her children in her drive to hurt and maintain control over their father, this is probably one of the hardest chapters of this book—hard for you to read and hard for us to write. Even though children are children, if Crazy has poisoned their relationship with their dad and they seem to be following in Crazy's footsteps, you must create and enforce boundaries with the kids, too. It may sound harsh to say, but there is really no kind way to put it.

Setting and maintaining healthy boundaries with children is a bare minimum for good parenting. Failing to recognize this and act on it is a form of psychological and emotional neglect that itself borders on abuse.

As parents and stepparents, it is your obligation to set the tone in your home and to have reasonable expectations on the conduct of children. That means zero tolerance for disrespect or abusiveness, especially when it is being orchestrated by Crazy using the kids. By tolerating the symptoms of alienation that Crazy has caused, you are only helping her infect the children further. It literally makes you her accomplice in the abuse.

It is up to you, as a couple, to see that Crazy is not rewarded for using her own children as pawns.

In extreme cases, this might mean saying the children right along with Crazy.

This is neither an option we suggest, nor one we v consider lightly. It is the last resort option after you l all other avenues. Before we get to what we consic ___ nuclear option, let's get the basics out of the way.

Having boundaries with your children is just good, basic parenting. Kids need rules and consistency, even children of divorce. There should be nothing shocking or groundbreaking about this. Children need parents, not peers, accomplices or enablers. Since Crazy likely acts as the latter rather than the former, it is up to the children's father and his partner to be the adult role models and parents in the truest sense of the word.

It is up to you to be the stepmother in whatever way that makes sense for your family, but being a stepmother who tolerates abuse from children, for whatever reason, is very hard to reconcile with the idea of making sense for your family. We have repeatedly stressed the importance of your husband standing up for himself and his new family. That also applies to you. Being a pushover for the antics of children whose minds have been poisoned is something you simply cannot do.

Kids test boundaries as part of healthy childhood development. Parents make the rules. Kids test and challenge the rules. Effective parents allow their kids to negotiate some of the rules when developmentally appropriate. When kids break non-negotiable rules, parents enforce natural consequences, discuss why that rule is important and why it isn't okay to break it. This is how kids learn appropriate, healthy behavior and how to function in a civilized society. Enforcing boundaries around kind and respectful behavior also helps children learn things like empathy, integrity and morality—three things Crazy typically lacks.

When you share children with Crazy, you may encounter difficulties unique to parenting with Crazy such as:

SAY GOODBYE TO CRAZY

Crazy is the "cool" mom or "fun" mom. Crazy is oftentimes more of a peer than a parent. This type of parenting abounds in social media memes like, "If you're not your child's best friend, you're doing something wrong." Actually, if you are your kid's best friend, you are most definitely doing something wrong. Crazy will turn her kids into her confidantes, therapists and surrogate spouse (i.e., parentification). Sometimes, Crazy will even party with her kids and supply alcohol and other drugs.

There is another term that can be used describe some or all of these behaviors. It is called *emotional incest*. This is where Crazy transfers the emotional needs she would normally have met by another adult to her children, putting them in the situation where they have to defend her in the same way one would defend a spouse or a lover. This is extremely abusive to children, and for many it will have a profoundly negative impact on their ability to form meaningful relationships as adults.

It also leaves discipline and healthy boundary enforcement to their father, who becomes the "not fun" parent. Crazy may even tell the kids that if you and their dad are being mean (i.e., enforcing healthy boundaries and rules), they can call her to come get them. Because of this, many dads and stepmoms are reluctant to set limits and consequences for bad behavior because their relationship with the kids is already strained, and dad's custody time is minimal. Speaking more frankly though, some readers of this book will be forced to make a decision on whether they want to be popular parents or good parents. We are betting that almost all will choose being good over being popular.

- **Crazy encourages and rewards the kids for acting out while with their father.** This is a tough one that puts you even more at cross-purposes with Crazy. You and your husband are trying to model and foster healthy behaviors and attitudes as well as have a loving relationship with the kids. Crazy, on the other hand, basically tells the kids being hateful and disrespectful to their father demonstrates their love and loyalty to her. Essentially, Crazy teaches the kids it's okay to be an asshole toward people with whom you are angry or don't like. This is a double bind for the kids—be punished while with dad for being disrespectful and hateful or be punished by Crazy for not being hateful and disrespectful toward their dad.

Keep in mind though that this is not a double bind that you created. In the end, good parenting on your part will have to supersede the confusion created by Crazy. Be frank with them. Tell them you understand the struggle they face, but that your house rules prohibit disrespectful and hateful behavior. End of story.

- **Two homes, two sets of rules.** This is to be expected in divorced and blended families. When dealing with an ex who isn't crazy, any discrepancies are probably minimal and not a big deal. When you share kids with Crazy, the difference in house rules can seem like going from Vegas to San Quentin. If Crazy is the cool mom or the "too self-absorbed to bother mom," the children may have very few rules or responsibilities, such as basic chores, cleaning up after themselves, etc. When they spend time with you, it can be a culture shock that takes them time to adjust to. Consistency on your part will help with that.

Whatever the bad behavior, there is a simple yardstick you can use if you are reluctant or unsure about setting a boundary and delivering a consequence. Ask yourselves if you would hesitate to discipline the children if Crazy were not part of the equation? And, for the stepmoms reading this, would you tolerate the same behavior from your own children? If the answers to both of these questions are no, then you are obligated as a parent to address these issues.

Hopefully, your issues with the kids can be managed by consistent boundary reinforcement and loving but firm discussions about behavioral expectations. Unfortunately, in many cases, this is not enough. Extreme cases of alienation and acting out may require therapeutic intervention, that is, if you can get a family court judge to acknowledge it, order it and enforce it.

If you are unable to get the kids into effective treatment, you may well have some tough choices ahead. They are choices that involve saying goodbye to your kids, at least for a time. Some of this we have already gone over in previous chapters. Now, we want you to ask·yourself some questions to determine if you have done all you can before making this very painful and difficult choice.

- Is the child an adult or a minor? If he or she is a minor, is he or she old enough to know right from wrong? For example, a 14-year old should know that it is wrong to be deliberately disrespectful and cruel, however a 3-year old child may not understand.

- If the child is a minor, have you done your best to get them psychological help to undo the damage done by Crazy?

- Does your local family court support you getting help for your child or is the judge allowing Crazy to determine treatment or not enforcing his or her own orders?

- If you have been able to get your child into therapy, is it effective? Does the therapist understand what is happening? Or is the therapist another negative advocate for Crazy?

- Have you consulted with an attorney about what is required to find a therapist for your child who will work toward undoing the alienation, instead of enabling and colluding with Crazy?

- Do you have the cooperation and understanding of other court appointees in your efforts to get help for yourself and the children such as the parenting coordinator or the guardian ad litem?

- If called, will the local police enforce your custody orders, or do they tell you that you need to take Crazy back to court?

- Have you acknowledged, owned and tried to make amends for any mistakes or hurts that you have made in your relationship with the child? Sometimes part of a child's anger is legitimate. If so, you need to own it and address it.

- Have you explicitly told the child that his or her behavior is hurtful or inappropriate? In other words, have you tried to establish boundaries and rules of acceptable engagement?

- If you have established clear boundaries, have you specified natural and meaningful consequences when he or she encroaches on your boundaries? For example, "I love you. You are my daughter, but it is unacceptable for you to insult my wife and me, refuse to see me and then expect me to pay for your college tuition." Or, "I love you. You are my son, but I will no longer tolerate you treating me with disrespect."

- Does your child treat you worse when you try to establish healthy boundaries? For example, does he or she think you're being abusive, controlling, over-sensitive, etc., for wanting to be treated with basic kindness, consideration, respect and civility? Does he or she try to portray you as the "bad dad" or "wicked stepmom" for not wanting to tolerate his or her abuse?

- Instead of honoring your reasonable requests to improve his or her behavior toward you, does the child tell others that there's something wrong with you and that you're the one who needs help?

If the children are adults, there may be nothing you can do to get them into therapy or to even see their father, for that matter. A judge cannot order a 23-year old to attend family therapy. With adult children, all you can really do is tell them your side of the story (without bashing Crazy), set boundaries, reach out to them periodically and hope they may someday come around, while accepting that they might not ever come around—unless they want something like money.

If the children are minors, are extremely alienated and you cannot get them the help they need, and they refuse to see their father or will only see him on their terms, it may be time for a difficult conversation. For example, perhaps your husband decides to stop seeking to enforce visitation through the courts. He can send an email early in the week asking if his 14-year old daughter plans to come for weekend visitation. If he receives no reply or a last minute reply in which she expects you to drop everything and change your plans—don't. Tell her you would love to see her, but you have plans now. Will Crazy use this against you and tell daughter that her father doesn't really love her? Sure, but it also tells daughter she's not in charge of visitation anymore.

Your children should not be calling the shots for your family any more than Crazy should.

To say this choice isn't easy is an enormous understatement. This is the kind of conversation and decision that can leave you both choking on Daddy and Stepmom Guilt. It's common for stepmoms to blame themselves for problems with the children. Fathers blame themselves for either divorcing Crazy or for not recognizing Crazy undermining him as a parent long before the divorce. Stepmoms may blame their husbands for not taking charge. A husband may resent his wife pointing out the problems and wanting him to do something about it.

There is more than enough guilt and blame to go around—some of it well placed, some of it displaced. Guilt and blame, however, do not solve the problem. Since Crazy is unlikely to stop the hatred and poisoning of the children, that means if things are going to get better it will be up to you and your husband. Sometimes *getting better* means letting the children go, as painful as that is.

You both have to decide how much more you are willing to tolerate, what your boundaries are and how to make peace individually and together with such a heartbreaking decision.

You may want to seek therapy, jointly, individually or both, with a counselor who has experience with these issues. Not all therapists are able to do this work. There are some therapists who will advise you to continue to allow yourselves to be abused indefinitely or until Crazy or the kids tire of it. On the other hand, you do not want a therapist who is too quick to suggest disengagement from the children. Making this decision is a grieving process all on its own.

If you make this gut wrenching choice, we encourage you to periodically reach out to the kids, whether they're adults or minors, to let them know you love them and hope to have a healthy, loving relationship with them someday, but, ultimately, the ball is in their court.

This part is as critical as it is simple. It is critical to let your children know that you are there with open arms as long as the rules are being followed—as long as you, your partner and everyone in your home is treated with respect. Let them know, as emphatically as is necessary, that this is not negotiable.

You can tell them that you sympathize with how hard their mother is making it to not choose sides, even as you tell them that choosing sides and acting out on it is not, nor will it ever be, acceptable. And then, as a good parent, you have to follow through.

Takeaways

- Setting boundaries with alienated children can be incredibly difficult. Administering appropriate discipline may alienate the children further.

- Allowing the children to be disrespectful and act out will not mend the damage done by Crazy. It teaches the children that their behavior is okay.

- Loving your children means instilling values and teaching them appropriate behavior. In other words, as the parent, it is your job to lead by example and be a grown-up.

- Setting healthy boundaries with your alienated kids might mean you will lose them for a time. This is an extremely tough choice, but in many cases, a necessary one.

Chapter 28

The Three D's:
Detach, Disengage, Defend

As we mentioned in a previous chapter, the mental health field often turns a blind eye or enables abusive women who use their children to continue to abuse and control an ex-husband and, by extension, his new family. "But she's The Mother of His Children" or "She has problems" or "She has BPD" seem to have become licenses to behave abusively.

They are not. Anyone who tells you otherwise is an enabler of the highest order, and the only thing following their advice is likely to get you is more Crazy.

These therapeutic enablers and apologists advise abuse victims of individuals with BPD to practice "radical acceptance" of the disorder and to "reframe their expectations." If you have chosen to stay in a relationship with a disordered person, then yes, you do need to accept that they are what they are and lower your expectations for being treated with consistent kindness and decency. Otherwise, you will forever be disappointed and surprised by their recurring abuse.

Or, as we heard one man quip regarding therapists who enable Crazy, "Borderlines go to therapy because it teaches them a language to justify the awful things they do to other people."

If you have decided to end your relationship with Crazy, the only thing you have to "radically accept" is that Crazy is *crazy*, it is unlikely that she will change and if you want peace and stability in your life you must learn to protect yourself from her. You don't have to accept her abuse. You don't have to bow down and submit because she is the bearer of the Golden Uterus or because she may or may not have a personality disorder. You don't have to tolerate her nonsense because your husband made the unfortunate choice of marrying and/or reproducing with her. It is time to stop letting the inmates run the asylum. Better yet, it's time for you to leave the asylum altogether.

Yes, mental illness is a serious issue. But remember, Crazy is not crazy in the sense that she doesn't know the difference between right and wrong and, therefore, cannot be held responsible for her actions. Crazy typically knows the difference between right and wrong, but operates under the belief that it's different when she does it, or that her bad behavior is justified because she's feeling hurt, jealous, abandoned, insecure or whatever slight she is feeling at any given moment. Now that we have explained the ABC's of Crazy, it's time to learn the Three D's.

The Three D's

There are three fundamental skills you will need to master in order to say goodbye to Crazy. These skills are the foundation blocks to many of the solutions and strategies discussed in this book.

The Three D's are:

- Detach.
- Disengage.
- Defend.

Detach. *Expect* the Crazy, but don't be *affected* by the Crazy. For the purposes of this book, emotional detachment is defined as the conscious choice not to allow another person to push your buttons, hurt, anger, frustrate or annoy you. The easiest way to do this is to develop indifference.

While it's natural to be angry with or even hate someone who has hurt you repeatedly, hate and anger gives Crazy power over you, your emotions and your life. Emotionally detaching from Crazy and her drama, power plays and intrusions will help to preserve your sanity. Even if you become a Crazy-busting Jedi Knight, Crazy will occasionally infiltrate your space and try to disturb your peace. The level of disturbance can be greatly reduced by how detached you are.

Much of Crazy's behavior is a form of attention seeking. She wants to get a rise out of you, so do not give it to her. This will be hard at first. Crazy could probably get the Dalai Lama to lose his cool. If emotional detachment is too difficult at first, then think of it as practicing the joy of withholding. A little schadenfreude as you watch her panic over failed attempts to get under your skin is fine, provided you understand the ultimate goal is actual, real detachment.

You know that Crazy is crazy. She is unlikely to change. Life will become much easier once you accept this and are able to put her behaviors in the proper perspective. A large part of her power over you is her ability to manipulate you into fear and anger.

As you detach and learn to ignore Crazy's antics (at least the non-life threatening, get you arrested and child endangering ones) Crazy will often become crazier in an effort to get your attention and maintain her control. When this happens, do not hit the panic button. Sit back and watch Crazy spin like a whirling dervish on meth with an amused smile as you and your partner relax in your Fortress of Reason.

Disengage. *Expect* the Crazy, but don't be *directed* by the Crazy. Crazy is often a button pusher and manipulator extraordinaire. Baiting you or your husband into engaging with her on her terms is a win for her. Crazy excels at anger and drama. When it comes to craziness, she has the home court advantage.

Therefore, only engage with Crazy on *your terms*. Crazy enjoys a good tug of war, so drop the rope and watch her fall on her ass without a push-pull partner. Crazy will still continue to be Crazy, but let her do it on her own.

In other words, limit your communication with and exposure to Crazy. Insulate yourself from her as best you can, and keep all interactions to a business-like bare minimum. Disengaging from the conflict and drama is like removing Crazy's fish hooks from your life and is a key to parallel parenting, which we will discuss in *chapter 29.*

Defend. *Expect* the Crazy, but don't *accept* the crazy behavior. If you want peace and stability in your home you need to strictly adhere to your boundaries and defend them. Crazy sees boundaries as both a threat and a challenge. She will seek out chinks in your armor and zero in on them. Let your boundaries slip even once, and you will be back to square one.

This means you cannot be flexible with the custody schedule, even if it means you miss out on things with the children. Remember— if you give Crazy an inch, she'll make a grab for your kidneys. Establish your boundaries and don't budge. It's unfortunate, but it's just the way it is.

Until the children age out, Crazy is your adversary. That may sound extreme, but we told you from the very beginning of this book that we were not going to sugarcoat reality. You may not wish to be locked in battle with Crazy, but Crazy is always at war with someone or something. Therefore, you need to identify and understand what drives your Crazy, so you can better protect yourself from her and implement effective consequences for her bad behavior.

Does she enjoy winding people up? Is she attention-seeking? Is she jealous? Is she driven by one of the five basic fears? For example, you might be able to leverage Crazy's fear of abandonment to induce appropriate behavior by giving her limited contact rather than ignoring her altogether. Alternately, if your Crazy is driven by the fear of loss of control, you can give her control over things that don't matter to you and don't harm the children like the color of their backpacks or who cuts the kids' hair.

Sometimes we learn the most from our mistakes. Here is an example of a family that did not practice the Three D's. The parties involved are Susan (the wife and stepmom), Dave (her husband), Crazy (the

ex-wife) and Stepdaughter (Dave and Crazy's 13-year old daughter).
Susan explains:

> Father's Day is coming. What does the new wife do for a
> dad whose child is being alienated from him by his ex? My
> daughter (from my first marriage) and I had a day planned
> for him. We wanted to take him to a classic car show as
> a surprise. He only knows we had an event planned that
> required tickets, not what the event is. This meant I needed
> to know if Stepdaughter would be joining us ahead of time
> instead of the last minute notice we usually get.
>
> Even though Dave gets Father's Day in his custody
> agreement, Crazy claims Stepdaughter doesn't want to see
> her dad because she feels 'uncomfortable' with us and Crazy
> says she will not force her to see us, but that's another story!
>
> Dave texted Stepdaughter and Crazy and we didn't hear back
> for a few days. Dave texted again and asked them to please
> respond by a specific time. We didn't get a response until
> later the next day when Crazy called Dave to scream at him
> for other things not related to Father's Day. She concluded
> by saying, "And you make your daughter respond to you on
> a timeline!" as if that is unreasonable when we are trying to
> plan a time sensitive event.
>
> Dave said, "I didn't get any response to my first text," to
> which Crazy yelled, "That's your answer!" Huh? So we
> can't ask for a timely response because we have to wait for
> no response? When we do that, it usually results in us having
> to reschedule things at the last minute or missing out on fun
> things we want to do as a family.
>
> The day after the call from Crazy, Dave said we "blocked"
> Stepdaughter out of spending Father's Day with us. I feel
> like he's giving in to Crazy's crazy logic again. Stepdaughter
> and her crazy-ass mom blocked her out of spending the day
> with us. We were trying to make plans to include her.

I am left with the impression that Dave thinks we did some injustice to Stepdaughter by asking her for a timely response. I know he feels really bad. What do I do? I could proceed with the car show, but I feel like it will be a sad event for him to celebrate without his daughter. Or I can give him some movie tickets and a gift card to his favorite restaurant and tell him to celebrate with Stepdaughter the next time he sees her and not celebrate Father's Day altogether.

This is a textbook example of Daddy Guilt and what happens when you do not practice the Three D's with Crazy. First, Dave needs to decide if he wants to continue to let Crazy control his relationship with their daughter and, if not, start to enforce his custody order. This may involve calling the cops if Crazy withholds visitation and taking her to court. Odds are Stepdaughter feels "uncomfortable" in her father's home because Crazy is making Stepdaughter "uncomfortable" if she has ever expressed any desire to see her father. If he had been enforcing the custody order all along, this might not have become an issue.

Second, Dave needs to set boundaries and enforce them with his daughter in spite of his Daddy Guilt. It is reasonable to ask for a timely response, especially when you need to schedule certain things in advance like purchasing tickets. Dave needs to keep requesting a respond-by time. If Stepdaughter blows it off, he should make plans without her. If Stepdaughter waits until the last minute to let her father know she wants to see him, his response should be, "I'm sorry, sweetheart, but when we didn't hear from you, we made plans to go to the car show, a party, etc. Next time, please get back to us in a timely manner so we can include you." No one respects a doormat, including children.

Stepdaughter, coached by Crazy, will undoubtedly play victim, but she will hopefully get the message that the world does not revolve around her, and that she is required to show respect and consideration if she wants to be included in family activities.

Third, Dave is displacing his anger and the blame. It's easier to blame Susan for the tensions between him, his daughter and his ex then it is to admit he married and bred with Crazy and that their daughter seems to be following in her mother's footsteps. While it is devastating to watch your own flesh and blood be taught to hate and abuse you, sticking his head in the sand and blaming Susan is not going to make the problem any less real.

Additionally, avoiding reality and deluding himself that Susan is to blame for the problems is hurting and fostering resentment in Susan. Dave would probably benefit from therapy with a therapist who understands these issues and by learning the importance of boundaries and the dangers of being a people-pleasing doormat.

Susan would also do herself a favor to flatly refuse to entertain any idea that she or David did anything wrong in this situation, and to not do anything compensatory for what were wrongful actions on the part of the ex and the daughter.

The above example does not have to be your life. Follow the Three D's, and put Crazy in her proper perspective in regards to your family.

Takeaways

- You do not have to allow Crazy to behave in a crazy fashion just because she's Crazy.

- Use the Three D's to bring peace and harmony into your life.

- Detach—Expect Crazy, but don't be affected by Crazy.

- Disengage—Expect Crazy to be crazy, but don't let her drive your bus

- Defend—Expect Crazy, but do not accept her crazy behavior.

- Follow the court order explicitly. Don't deviate. She won't reciprocate, and Crazy will see it as a weakening in your boundaries.

- Until the kids age out of the court system, Crazy is your adversary.

Chapter 29

Parallel Parenting: Because You Cannot Co-Parent with Crazy

Co-parenting after divorce can be challenging—even for psychologically healthy individuals. It requires that you and your ex communicate and work together whether or not you disagree or plain old just dislike one another. You set aside your differences, realize that the kids deserve a loving relationship with both of their parents, let go of the resentments from when you were together (or at least keep your mouth shut about it), raise the kids and get on with your lives.

Effective co-parenting requires emotional maturity, understanding that your way is neither the only way nor the best way, shielding the children from parental conflict as best you can, rather than putting them in the middle of it, and doing what is in the best interests of the children. Just to be clear, the "best interests of the children" are not automatically synonymous with the mother's best interests, her agenda and/or her feelings. It is usually in the best interests of the children to have equal access, by way of 50/50 custody, to two loving parents. Crazy has serious limitations in this regard that make it difficult, if not impossible, to co-parent with her.

Crazy does not compromise unless there is something in it for her. Crazy does not cooperate unless there is something it for her. Crazy does not share unless there is something in it for her. Crazy believes court orders are optional, at least as they apply to her.

Crazy believes she knows best on all child-related matters. She views the children's love for their father as an act of disloyalty and a threat to the children's love for her. Crazy requires, implicitly and/or explicitly, that the children take sides and choose her. She

...lerstand that children can love both parents without it ...their love for her.

...the children are another item to be won in the divorce settlement. She knows full well that the children are often the easiest and most effective way to hurt, manipulate and control her ex. Under Crazy's tutelage, the children can become weapons, hostages held for ransom and/or foot soldiers in her campaign of hate.

Crazy's definition of co-parenting seems to be, "I make all the decisions. Dad does whatever I tell him to do and is grateful for whatever time I allow him to have with *my* children." Much like when your husband was married to Crazy, she still expects him to take orders from her. Therefore, expecting Crazy to co-parent or trying to co-parent with Crazy is, in and of itself, *crazy*.

Post-Divorce Conflict Is More Damaging to Children Than Divorce

Parental conflict that continues *after* the divorce has been finalized causes more harm to children than the divorce itself. Children exposed to conflict, both in marriage and after divorce, are at greater risk for developing emotional problems, relationship problems, social problems, academic problems and substance abuse problems.[21] Therefore, reducing parental conflict is perhaps the most important thing parents can do to help their children adjust during and after divorce.[22]

Most people divorce to end unresolvable marital conflict, not so with Crazy. Crazy *loves* conflict and wants it to go on and on and on. When children are involved, divorcing Crazy rarely ends the conflict, it just changes the playing field. Since Crazy refuses to see the damage she does and either cannot or will not change her abusive, controlling, intrusive and other high-conflict behaviors, it is up to your husband and you to minimize the conflict—for the children's sake[23] and for the sake of your marriage. Parallel parenting is the most effective way to reduce ongoing parental conflict with Crazy.

Adopting a parallel parenting approach means you will essentially parent *around* Crazy rather than *with* Crazy, which we have already established is unlikely to work. The three basic components of parallel parenting are low or minimal contact, clear boundaries and a highly specific custody agreement. Crazy eats lazy lawyer, boilerplate custody agreements for breakfast, so it is essential to have a custody order that leaves nothing open for interpretation by either parent.

If effectively structured, a parallel parenting plan provides parents and children with predictability and consistency and can prevent future conflict.[24] It should alleviate the need to negotiate parenting issues *after* the divorce, which is one way Crazy keeps the conflict going. Any parenting agreement should be seen as a living document that will change as the children grow and change, so you may need to revise it periodically.

Depending on the number of children involved and other variables, a parallel parenting agreement can be anywhere from 30 to 80+ pages long. It should cover education, medical and mental health, right of first refusal, vacations, extracurricular activities and how communication between the parents will be handled. We recommend OurFamilyWizard, a third party communication system that, if used properly, can become a running affidavit.[25] Other topics that should be covered by this agreement include emergencies, including how to handle deaths in the family and medical emergencies, and special events such as family weddings, graduations. You should also include third party childcare, including background checks, visitation with extended family, how custody exchanges will be handled, religious practices, diet and any other potential sources of conflict. It's also important to include how you will make updates to the parenting plan. The goal is to troubleshoot any opportunities for Crazy to make mischief regarding the children and have a clear protocol in writing.

In our experience, Crazy does not like parallel parenting. She tends to see it as "controlling," even though the agreement applies to *both* parents. The goal of a parallel parenting plan is not to *control* Crazy, but to *contain* Crazy's crazy in order to reduce the

e generates that is damaging to the children. An effective
arenting plan implements boundaries, accountability and
nces—three things Crazy hates.

Commonly, Crazy will argue that her ex only wants to parallel parent
to "get her in trouble." In reality, neither parent will get in trouble if
they are both behaving and abiding by the mutually binding parallel
parenting agreement. The parent who refuses to parallel parent is
basically admitting that they are going to ignore boundaries and
misbehave.

Crazy may also argue that parallel parenting will harm the children
because mom and dad should be able to communicate without
any restrictions and/or insist upon face-to-face time with the other
parent *for the sake of the children.* Yes, mom and dad should be able
to communicate without a 40-page document detailing how they
will communicate, but that would require Crazy not to be crazy. In
reality, "Children can be well-adjusted regardless of whether their
parents adopt cooperative or parallel parenting, or some blend of the
two, as long as conflicts are kept to a minimum, there is responsible
parenting at both homes, and legal agreements clearly specify
custody, schedules, and decision-making arrangements."[26]

It would also be great for the kids to see mom and dad interact in
a friendly fashion after the divorce. However, Crazy typically uses
face-time to put her ex on the spot. For example telling Dad in front
of the children, "I told the kids I want to take them to Six Flags on
your day next week because that is the only time I can take them,
and they really want to go!" Another example is hitting her ex up
for money, in addition to court-ordered child/spousal support, as an
opportunity to create conflict. Since Crazy frequently abuses face
time and open communication with her ex, the boundaries parallel
parenting provides are necessary to say goodbye to Crazy.

Takeaways

- You cannot co-parent with Crazy.

- Crazy doesn't want to co-parent with you, either, no matter what she might say. She only wants to parent the way she wants to with no input from anyone else.

- Crazy enjoys the conflict, and doesn't care that the kids are hurt by ongoing conflict.

- Parallel parenting is parenting around Crazy. She won't want to do this, and she may even claim it harms the children. Remember that sole parenting is always her goal and ignore any bait she tosses out other than to refute her claims of harm.

- You will need to get a very detailed and specific parallel parenting plan. This will afford the children with stability and consistency. It can also minimize future conflict.

- Crazy will fight any efforts you make to change the parenting plan.

Chapter 30

Communication: Less is More

When it comes to communicating with Crazy, less is definitely more. Less contact means less conflict, which is ultimately in the best interests of the children, and in the best interests of your relationship and overall well-being. Since Crazy typically thrives on drama, chaos and anger, she won't be very happy about less contact. Alternately, there is another kind of Crazy who will refuse to communicate with you, which can pose its own set of challenges. However, if you're dealing with the latter kind of Crazy and not the former, count your blessings and be grateful. In case you didn't already know, a little Crazy goes a *long* way.

We assume that you are dealing with the Crazy who looks for any reason to communicate with your husband or manufactures reasons to communicate. *The toilet is overflowing—what do I do? YOUR son won't do his homework. The cat coughed up a hairball. Did you send this month's child support check (*this one's especially funny when Crazy is having your paycheck garnished by the state and it arrives in her mailbox, like clockwork, the same day each and every month)?*

Perhaps you get the long, rambling insult-filled emails with one or two legitimate child questions buried within the nasty-gram. Maybe your Crazy uses text messaging as if it were a rapid-fire assault rifle. Or maybe she leaves countless voicemails demanding that your husband call her back because its an "*EMERGENCY!*" but neglects to mention the nature of the emergency. If you haven't figured it out yet, your definition of *emergency* and Crazy's definition of "*EMERGENCY!*" are probably very different. Being ignored or not getting her way is what usually constitutes an "*EMERGENCY!*" for Crazy.

Why does Crazy insist on unnecessary and often intrusive communication? Much of it has to do with the five basic fears that drive Crazy, particularly staving off feelings of abandonment and wanting to maintain her sense of control and power over your husband and, subsequently you. Contact is also how Crazy maintains the spell of fear, obligation and guilt she casts over her targets and practices abusive behaviors like gaslighting. Face-to-face or phone contact is most effective in this capacity, which is one of the reasons we recommend all communication be in writing whenever possible.

As previously discussed, we recommend adopting a parallel parenting approach, officially or unofficially. One of the main principles of parallel parenting is low contact, which means very little communication—the least amount possible. It is relatively simple to minimize contact if your husband or his attorney had the presence of mind to insist on a highly detailed custody agreement when he and Crazy divorced that clearly spells out how educational, medical and mental health decisions, extracurricular activities, sports, holidays, splitting the costs of extracurricular activities, medical reimbursement, insurance, school tuition and how communication will be handled.

If your Crazy uses her phone to bombard you with insults, baseless accusations, questions you know she already has the answer to, to wind the kids up and otherwise intrude on your husband's parenting time, going low contact can spare you a lot of headaches once you get the hang of it. It will be difficult at first, especially if your husband still fears Crazy and has been trained to reply as soon as she commands, or if he still feels the need to defend himself or reason with Crazy.

Going low contact means that all unnecessary communication with Crazy comes to a screeching halt. Believe it or not, much of the communication you're having with Crazy is probably unnecessary. Not every email or text requires a response. In fact, with Crazy, we would be willing to wager that 95% of her communications require no reply whatsoever.

Most communications from Crazy are:

- **Attention seeking**. Crazy wants to make sure your husband hasn't forgotten about her. Good attention, bad attention—it doesn't matter. For Crazy, bad breath, as the old saying goes, is better than no breath. Crazy will attempt to stir up conflict, engage you in defensive back and forth, manufacture kid dramas, etc.

- **Attempts to ascertain if she still has control**. Will her ex still react when she yanks his chain? Sometimes Crazy floats out test balloons just to see if she can elicit a response.

- **Bogus documentation for court**. Crazy lies or distorts issues with the kids believing that if she sends an email stating that the kids are failing school and it's all your husband's fault (even when the kids are with her during the school week when it is her responsibility to make sure they are doing their homework) or that the children have told her that you, the evil stepmom, walk around naked and it makes the children "uncomfortable" (in reality, you wore a modest bikini to a pool party) it will be seen as gospel truth in court.

- **Money grubbing**. Oftentimes, Crazy believes she is entitled to more money than her ex is court ordered to pay her. It is common to receive angry, whiny or desperate emails from Crazy claiming her electricity or heat is about to be shut off, she can't afford to fix the plumbing and what kind of father would let his children suffer without electricity?! That's your husband's cue to offer to let the children stay with the two of you while Crazy sorts out her financial mess. If she can't take care of the problem, the answer isn't to give Crazy money for a problem that may or may not exist. You remove the children from the situation.

- **Attempts to cause disruption**. Crazy wants to swap custody time. Can she have the kids on your time because there's a super special event that is only occurring during your custody time, and if the kids don't get to go they will be *scarred for life!!!* Or she schedules a crisis the day before you are scheduled to take the kids on vacation.

Going low or no contact, like any other boundary you set with Crazy, will most likely cause her to initially push back. Hard. Brace yourselves and prepare for the angry, guilt-inducing, bad parent accusations and other attempts to engage you in pointless communication to escalate for a time.

Also remind yourself that if you are detached in a healthy way, none of that will matter.

The most important reason to have as little contact with Crazy as possible is because *your goal is to say goodbye to Crazy*. You do that by limiting communication and maintaining a healthy distance, both unmistakable signs of detachment.

How to go low contact:

Put it in writing. Terminate any connections you have on social media like Facebook. Insist that all communication is via email or SMS. Since Crazy is high-conflict, it likely means you will need to go back to court to have orders enforced, work with a guardian ad litem or hire a parenting coordinator. Written communication creates a paper trail that verbal communication cannot duplicate, even if you are recording. If you must have verbal communication—always be recording (ABR)—otherwise it is he said-she said.

Written communication also gives you time to pause and identify Crazy's manipulations or agenda rather than giving her an immediate, emotional response. For most people, it's often easier to identify Crazy's ploys, lies, diversionary tactics, etc., if you read them, feel whatever emotions arise and then go back and identify her game. Sometimes talking to Crazy in real time is like talking to the snake in *The Jungle Book*—her eyes turn into spinning kaleidoscopes and you find yourself buying into the most unbelievable garbage or losing your cool.

Kids only. If your husband has a decent custody order, the only reason to communicate with Crazy are child-related issues, such as sending receipts, reimbursement, doctor's appointments, school issues or running late for an exchange. The *only* reason to have telephone/verbal contact is a child-related emergency. As we already noted, what you and your husband consider a child emergency and what Crazy considers an *"EMERGENCY!"* are probably two very different things. If you make a commitment to only discuss relevant issues, it makes it easier not to get sucked into Crazy traipsing down *Memory Blame*, the Shame Game, name-calling or whatever else she likes to do.

The 3 B's. Not all Crazies are alike, but a good number love, love, love drama. They can create a national emergency out of a paper cut. If you don't respond immediately with the utmost concern, they will label you a neglectful, bad parent. *But…the paper cut could get infected! They might have to amputate your daughter's index finger! What kind of father are you?!?!*

A good rule of thumb for what constitutes a true child emergency are the 3 B's. Blood. Broken bones. Brain damage. Even if there is a medical emergency, you can still text or email. For example, "Jonathan fell off the monkey bars and cut his knee. Heading to St. Matthew's ER for stitches. Will text you doctor's prognosis." If your husband has done a good of job of insisting that coaches, teachers and doctors send him duplicate information, there is no reason to use Crazy as a conduit for child-related information—especially if she likes to withhold information, and many of them do, to cause mischief and exert control over you.

BIFF (Brief, Informative, Firm, ~~Friendly~~). Most communication should be no more than one to five sentences maximum. Try not to send messages that cover more than two issues. Stick to information and the facts. Do not express emotion or discuss Crazy's emotions. Do not criticize Crazy's parenting (document your concerns in a journal and then, if need be with an attorney and/or the court) or offer Crazy parenting advice or suggestions, which she will likely perceive as criticism. The shorter your messages are, the less material you give Crazy to twist and distort.

Write every email or reply to Crazy's communications as if a judge will be reading it. Do not take Crazy's bait when she implies you are a bad parent or a jerk and send a two-page defense of yourself. You need to learn to let her insults and insinuations roll off your back and do NOT respond in kind. You may have noticed we struck "Friendly" from BIFF. Crazy is not your friend, so do not treat her as such. If your Crazy has diffuse boundaries or no boundaries, even a mildly friendly tone can be an invitation to test the boundaries you are trying to enforce. Try to achieve a business-like tone. Civil, not friendly.

The 48-Hour Rule. One of the most difficult things for many individuals to learn is that not every message from Crazy requires a response. One lingering result of being in an abusive relationship with Crazy is that your husband may have become conditioned to replying immediately to every single one of Crazy's emails, texts or calls. This needs to stop.

A good way to ride out the anxiety of giving an immediate response is to implement a 48-hour rule. Do not reply to any non-emergency communication until after 48 hours or more have passed, that is, if a response is required at all. This gives any sense of conditioned urgency time to dissipate and dismantles one of Crazy's control levers. It will also probably cause Crazy to ratchet up her attempts at communication.

Part of saying goodbye to Crazy is training her that only relevant, civil communication will get her a response. If she is unable or unwilling to learn this, she can rage into the void all by her lonesome.

Voicemail and Caller ID—Use Them. Crazy is why voicemail and caller ID were invented. **Let all phone calls from Crazy go to voicemail**. If she doesn't leave a message, don't call back. If she leaves a message telling you to call her but doesn't say why, don't call back. If she leaves a detailed message about a kid issue, do not call her back. Respond via email and ask that she use email for all future communications, but make her wait 72 hours or longer for the response instead of 48. It is the consequence for violating the boundary. Basically, do not reply to any kind of communication unless it is a legitimate kid emergency—blood, broken bones, brain damage.

Joint Email Account. If you are an involved stepparent, or your Crazy believes your husband is still her husband, it is important that you and your husband present a united front. Create a new email account for all Crazy communications, for example, MikeandSueJones@ yahoo.com. Do not reply to messages sent to individual accounts.

Create an auto-respond message that redirects Crazy to the new email address. The goal is to eliminate the "special connection" Crazy insists on maintaining with your husband. It also demonstrates that you are both on the same page, which will make it more difficult for Crazy to manipulate and play games with communication.

The Batshit Phone. If Crazy has too much free time on her hands and texts, calls or emails non-stop, and it's financially feasible, you may want to get a separate cellphone account just for Crazy. Many individuals who share kids with Crazy experience anxiety and dread whenever their cellphone rings or the SMS alert chimes. If you contain Crazy to her own device, you don't have to live in fear of the phone you use for family, friends and business anymore.

Stop Eating Shit Sandwiches. Oftentimes, Crazy will send what we call "shit sandwich" emails. In other words, there are one or two kernels of kid-related issues sandwiched in the middle of a whole bunch of shit. Focus on the actual questions or requests about the kids and ignore the rest. For example, *"We will be using all of the tickets to Son's graduation allotted to us by the school."* If you write one word more you're on the wrong track.

If Crazy sends a follow-up message to tell you how selfish you are and to hurl more insults, guilt trips or make more demands, ignore her. You don't reply after the initial response.

The Exception to the Rule. If Crazy accuses you, your husband or other family members of any kind of abuse or endangerment, you will need to reply. Accusations of neglect, abuse or endangerment should be responded to within a short time frame. Again, we recommend keeping it BIF. A simple, "Your allegations are not true," "That did not happen," "You are exaggerating what happened," etc., should suffice. Offline make sure you gather any evidence to show Crazy is lying in case you have to go to court or deal with Children's Protective Services.

Third Party Communication Systems. Sometimes you may be able to obtain a court order to use a third party communication system like OurFamilyWizard (OFW). These kinds of programs are the preferred system of communication when you are dealing with a high-conflict Crazy. If used properly, a communication platform like OFW can become your running affidavit. It is ultimately an accountability device for Crazy, which is why she will likely balk at using it and claim that you are trying to control her or "get her into trouble."

OFW busts Crazy on her communication gamesmanship. You can see when she has logged in and if she has opened your communications. Obviously, this impairs her ability to claim she didn't receive your email. Although, we know of cases in which certain Crazies still lie about this even though there is evidence to the contrary. OFW also offers shared parenting calendars and the capacity to upload receipts. If you are able to get an order to use OFW, do not use any other mode of communication. Containing Crazy to one mode of communication is best.

Takeaways

- Less communication is better. Crazy thrives on conflict. Less communication equals fewer opportunities to create conflict.

- Crazy won't like less communication. It's a boundary. Crazy doesn't do boundaries.

- If you can't go no contact, go low contact.

- Communicate only in writing. All calls go to voicemail. You must keep records of everything.

- Don't take the bait. Do not respond to her crazy or anything that does not legally require a response or is not about the children.

- Only exception to the rule—do not allow accusations of abuse or endangerment towards you or any family members to go unchallenged. A simple denial will suffice. Gather evidence to refute Crazy's claims offline. Do not engage in discussion.

Chapter 31

Know Thy Custody Order

Hopefully, when your husband's attorney drafted his custody order, he or she understood high-conflict custody cases and did *not* crank out a cookie cutter co-parenting order. When dealing with Crazy, those kinds of custody orders are about as effective as a tissue paper shield against a stampeding hoard of barbarians. They also practically guarantee your husband's enrollment in the Family Court Frequent Flyer program.

In the chapter on parallel parenting, we discussed the necessity of having a highly detailed custody order. A custody order that is vague, ambiguous or loosey-goosey is Crazy's playground. If there are items open for interpretation, they will be interpreted to mean what she wants them to mean. If there are loopholes, she will drive a Mack Truck through them.

Before we address the importance of knowing your custody order, we have some questions for you and your husband:

- **Are you and your husband happy with his custody order?** Is it specific enough? Does it troubleshoot problems in advance by effectively heading Crazy off at the pass? Is it clear enough for a fifth-grader to understand, as this is Crazy's average emotional age? Does it minimize unnecessary contact with Crazy?

- **Does your husband's attorney understand what parallel parenting is and does he or she have experience advocating for it?** If your husband's attorney blanches at the idea of parallel parenting, you may need to find another attorney, but first you need to understand why. Some attorneys, unbelievable given their line of work, don't have a clue about high-conflict cases and personality disorders.

Family law attorneys who are not up to speed on these issues are to be avoided at all costs because they are likely to cost you *a lot* in terms of money and your husband's children. They will tell you a parallel parenting plan will make you look controlling and punitive, ignoring the fact that you are legally obliged to follow it right along with Crazy. There are attorneys who understand and are in favor of parallel parenting, but they know the family court judge is not, which brings us to our next question.

- **Is your family court judge a Golden Uterus worshipper or woefully ignorant about the necessity of parallel parenting in high-conflict cases?** One of these conditions is bad enough. Being terminally mommy-biased and ignorant is the kiss of death for fathers in family court. This kind of judge will see your insistence on having a parallel parenting plan and minimal contact with Crazy as mean and controlling and view you as having an "unwillingness to communicate, cooperate and co-parent." *Oh, the irony.* A good attorney will most likely advise you that this kind of judge will only consider the custody order you need *after* you have demonstrated Crazy is an uncooperative scofflaw by returning to court repeatedly as she violates the useless custody order. Usually, after 18 months to 3 years and possibly tens of thousands of dollars in legal fees, you might be able to get a parallel parenting plan with this kind of judge. That is if the kids haven't been alienated into oblivion while Crazy has been unilaterally calling the shots under the original custody order. *Good times.*

- **Does your family court judge uphold his or her own orders?** In other words, even the most finely crafted parallel parenting plan is not worth the paper it is printed on if the judge does not enforce his or her own orders. It is important to know this so you do not waste your time and resources fighting a battle you are unlikely to win.

We hate to beat a crazy horse, but here's the deal: *Crazy is a boundary tester extraordinaire.* Because Crazy is chock full o' nuts, an effective custody order must be chock full o' boundaries. Sane people avoid going into the legal system if possible. Crazy salivates like one of Pavlov's dogs at the opportunity of donning her professional victim attire and putting on a show for the court.

This typically changes after Crazy gets her first good spanking by the judge—it can and does happen. There are some judges who will not tolerate Crazy's antics, or at least not for long. We hope you have one of those judges.

When we instruct you to know thy custody order, we don't mean have a general understanding of it. We don't mean know what desk drawer you have it tucked away in to consult when you think Crazy is pulling a fast one. We don't mean make stuff up as you go along that seems to be in the spirit of the custody order. No, no, no.

We mean be able to recite your custody order like an evangelical preacher quotes Bible Scripture. And do not deviate from the custody order. Ever.

Your custody order, provided your family court enforces its own orders, is one of your first lines of defense against Crazy. This is why it needs to be more than a paper shield. You want titanium steel.

Crazy usually doesn't follow rules—unless they're in her favor. Crazy makes up the rules as she goes along her crazy way. Sometimes Crazy will insist on a modification or deviation to the custody order one week, and the following week deny it happened. The fact that you have email correspondence that proves what actually happened is irrelevant to Crazy.

Oftentimes, Crazy believes just because she puts something in writing, say in an email or a text, it becomes fact and, in some really crazy cases, the law. Crazy is kind of like the Texas Board of Education in this respect. She rewrites and revises history at will. Things like the truth, reality, evidence and the facts are mere trifles to Crazy. She swats them away like a pesky mosquito.

Crazy will expect, nay—*demand*, that you make special exceptions to the custody order when she requires it. She can't possibly drive your husband's daughter to her court ordered therapy appointment because her second cousin's best friend's babysitter's grandmother's dog walker's husband died and she must, must, *must* be in attendance at the funeral. Did she know him? No, but she's just devastated, and her second cousin's best friend's babysitter's grandmother's dog walker *needs her* in her time of grief. *Good grief,* more like.

Therefore, your husband can either leave work an hour early, drive across town and do what Crazy has been court ordered to do, but doesn't want to do, or eat the 24-hour cancellation fee for their child's therapy session and miss out on repairing the damage Crazy has caused to his relationship with their daughter. Your husband, being a good father who loves his daughter and who wants her to get the help she needs, leaves work early. He gets docked for an hour's pay, thinking that, at some point, he will need a similar favor from Crazy.

Except that's not how Crazy works.

If your husband still believes the Golden Rule (i.e., the ethic of reciprocity) works with Crazy, he may be just as crazy as Crazy is. Either that, or he has a severe case of Charlie Brown-itis in which Lucy (aka Crazy) yanks the football away from him as he runs up to kick it. Every single time. Aaaaaaargh!

Several months later, when your husband's father dies, their daughter's paternal grandfather, and he asks Crazy to switch weekends with him so their daughter can attend the memorial service, Crazy tells him no, that is Crazy's parenting time. Or, she will use it as an opportunity to extort money. In order for their daughter to attend the funeral, he will end up having to pay her electric bill, for example, because she spent child support check on a new Coach bag.

No good deed goes unpunished with Crazy.

By the way, a good custody order will spell out how family deaths and emergencies are handled. We know the connection between Crazy's lack of financial responsibility and their daughter attending her grandfather's funeral has zero connection, but Crazy will find one.

Do not deviate from your custody order. It is another boundary, and it's just as important to enforce as your other boundaries with Crazy. In fact, unlike many of your personal boundaries with Crazy, your custody order boundaries are enforceable under the law, at least they should be.

Here's another example. Let's say your husband arrives to pick up the kids at his scheduled custody time, and Crazy tells him the kids don't want to go. This is his cue to tell her if she doesn't send the kids out he will call the police to enforce the custody order. And then he pulls out the copy he keeps in his glove box at all times.

The police may not enforce the order when they arrive, but your husband can ask for a report of the incident, which he can then take to the judge. We recommend handling Crazy's court order violations in clusters of three or four. You do not want to go to court for each and every custody order transgression, because that might make you look high-conflict, not to mention it can also be expensive, so stack them up.

As an aside, if your husband is still picking the kids up at Crazy's residence, we strongly recommend changing the location to a public place with surveillance cameras that's equidistant between Crazy's home and your home.

Custody order violations must be documented. Your attorney should be able to tell you the best way to document Crazy's violations to present to the court. It should be in a form that is easy for the judge to understand and does not require him or her to do a lot of paper shuffling or reading. Never underestimate the laziness and apathy of public officials, even the ones who are the supposed champions of the best interests of children.

If you are dealing with this kind of Crazy, your attorney should try to present a persistent pattern of consistent noncompliance to the judge over time. If your attorney can successfully do this, it might just get you a parallel parenting plan or primary custody, if that is what you want. Again, that is if your court is willing to uphold its own laws. Additionally, each time you have to haul Crazy back to court for order violations, your attorney should ask for your legal fees to be reimbursed by Crazy.

Your attorney may tell you or your husband that you'll never get fees because judges don't award fees to fathers, but insist on asking. You definitely won't get your legal fees reimbursed if you don't ask. You may not get them reimbursed the first, second, third, fourth or fifth time you ask, but you might at some point. And when you do, behold the mushroom cloud of Crazy. It will be *spectacular*.

She will wail and screech and gnash her teeth, as if she is being asked to pay with a literal pound of her flesh. It's okay for Crazy to rack up legal fees for her ex over her ridiculous motions, etc. It's not so fun when the very expensive shoe is on her foot. We think it looks *fabulous* on her.

Why are you doing this? Remember Crazy's big five fears that we discussed earlier. Crazy may never abide by the court orders, even if she experiences negative consequences. Sometimes Crazy is just too crazy (or stupid) to learn, even in the face of pain and punishment. Then there is the kind of Crazy who will knock the nonsense off, or at least lessen it for a time, if she is penalized through loss of money, loss of parenting time or just plain old losing in court. Losing in court doesn't jibe with her victim narrative. Crazy likes to win. Once she starts to lose at her own games they cease being fun for her.

Even if you don't ever get legal fees, if Crazy gets spanked enough by the judge (and sometimes one spanking is enough), Crazy may cop an attitude with the judge. Judges don't like that. Not even when women do it. If she exposes her true colors in family court that is very good for you.

If you don't know your custody order inside and out, you will have a more difficult time abiding by and enforcing it. You do not deviate from the custody order because doing so renders it meaningless, or more meaningless than Crazy already views it. Not deviating from your custody order, not making exceptions and not doing favors will also reduce contact with Crazy. Your goal is to get her to the point where she knows better than to ask.

It is also just as important to know your state, province or country custody laws. Here is a *link to a directory* with information for every US states' custody and *visitation laws* and *one for Canada*. It is helpful to know what your basic parenting rights are in your family court jurisdiction because Crazy may insist on things or threaten to take legal action against you regarding custody issues that are not covered under the law. You also want to know if state, provincial or territorial guidelines and laws supersede any agreements you and Crazy make between yourselves.

Takeaways

- Exercise boundaries with Crazy that are (or should be) enforceable under the law.

- Exercise boundaries and deliver appropriate negative consequences in order to say goodbye to Crazy.

- Protect, exercise and enforce your husband's parenting rights.

- Document Crazy's violations in the hopes of getting a more equitable custody order or a change in custody, if that's what you want.

Chapter 32

Getting Back on the Horse

It is our hope at this point in the book that you have made a transition in the way you are viewing and handling Crazy. By now we anticipate that you have accepted the idea that you cannot fight this alone and that a unified front—you and your partner working in tandem—is the only way forward that will make a real difference.

You and your husband or boyfriend have signed and committed to the couple's contract, and you are ready work as an indivisible team to evict Crazy from every possible aspect of your life.

As you step forward to restore the sanity to your home, you can be sure of two things. One, Crazy will test your resolve, especially in the beginning. Two, consistently, even if not perfectly, defeating her attempts to tear down your newly built walls is the key to your success.

That being said you are human and will make mistakes. Your husband or boyfriend is just as human and will make his own mistakes, as well. Doing your best is important. Expecting perfection out of yourself or anyone else, however, is not going to serve you very well. Your journey is of learning new behaviors, and in developing boundaries around your relationship and around yourself.

There will be missteps, and plenty of them. Weaknesses will rise to the surface and show themselves at inopportune times. Old habits will kick in without your even thinking about them. That means you will have setbacks from which you will have to learn. You will likely have several rounds of picking yourself up off the ground, dusting yourself off, and getting back on the horse.

This is a horse that will throw you. Get used to it, and remember what you have always heard in life. When you get thrown from a horse, the best thing to do is to get back on and ride!

Crazy as an Addiction

In the study of addictions, we find that smoking is a habit that is one of the toughest to tackle. In fact, nicotine it is harder to quit than most illicit drugs, including drugs like cocaine and heroin. Recent research indicates that on any given attempt to quit smoking only 4% to 7% people manage to do it. The research also indicates, however, that those who make persistent, dedicated attempts to quit are the most likely to ultimately prevail.

You have to view saying goodbye to Crazy with the same understanding and even more caution. After all, nicotine does not plot to make you relapse. Nicotine does not systematically learn your weaknesses and make trade of exploiting them. Nicotine does not scheme and manipulate. Nicotine does not attack your children or use them as pawns. Crazy does all these things. You have to be prepared.

Examine your Mistakes Without Being Defensive

The temptation can be overwhelming to blame Crazy for your mistakes. After all, it's perfectly normal to blame people whose life work is to make you miserable. The thing is, though, that objective self-analysis and accountability for your own actions will do more good than pointing fingers.

Consider the following scenario:

Crazy shows up at your home to pick up the kids two hours early from visitation with no warning, saying that she has to get them early because of a scheduling problem. She turns it into a scene when you resist. The children become upset over the drama and act out with some of it directed at you, because Crazy has made you the scapegoat in the eyes of the kids.

In this scenario it is easy to blame Crazy (she has that coming!) and to just spiral down into obsessing over her actions. It is difficult at that particular moment to start considering how you could have better handled the situation. After all, what could you do? She showed up at the door and caused a scene!

All of that is perfectly logical, sensible and does absolutely nothing to help you. Remember, getting Crazy to live in the world of logical and sensible is like trying to teach calculus to a chimpanzee. You might as well try to chisel through a block of granite with a toothpick.

The fact that you are absolutely in the right in this situation is similarly useless. Being right may be a great feeling, but it won't help you say goodbye to Crazy. In fact, you can get so stuck in the outrage of being simultaneously right and screwed that you miss golden opportunities to learn the larger lesson.

Rather than fulminate in your indignation or find someone to blame for the troubles, we suggest that you take a few deep breaths and go back to this scene with an eye for asking yourself a couple of the right questions.

What gave her the impression it was okay to come to your home? We have touched on this before. Crazy at your door will eventually be Crazy through your door. That does not jibe with the word *goodbye*. If your plan for Crazy so far has not included a ban on her from your front door, this is a good time to fix that with public drop-off/pickup locations. Tell your lawyer to make it happen.

Why did you answer the door? It is a legit question. Most people don't answer their door unless they know who is knocking. When you are saying goodbye to Crazy you must always know who is knocking. If it's Crazy who's there two hours early, there is absolutely no need for you to open the door. What you can do is advise Crazy—through the door—to check the text messages on her phone where she should find the following, which you just sent:

"You need to leave the property. We will meet you at (public location) at the prescribed time. The next call we make is to the police."

That is it. That is all you have to say. Then, if she does not leave, you call and have her removed by police. Record everything and get a report and case number from the police.

There are other questions you should ask yourself throughout this process. Are you detached in a healthy way? Are you remaining thoughtful and deliberate in your actions, or are you just pissed at Crazy and reacting? If possible, did you enlist the support and help of your partner through this event? Did he provide that support? If not, how did you handle that? Have you taken action to legally restrain Crazy from being on your property? If not, why? Do yourself a favor and make sure you answer all those questions honestly and accurately. Remember, it is the questions you ask yourself and your partner that matter here, not the questions you have about Crazy.

In the beginning Crazy will quickly see that you are moving in a different direction, one with which she is not very pleased. It will become her mission to derail you as quickly as possible. Her alienation antics may well go into high gear. She will test limits more to see how far she can go and to erode your resolve. She will try to do anything to create division between you and your partner. She knows very well that breaking the ties that bind you and your partner will make your house tumble down around her feet, which is exactly what she wants. It is what she has always wanted.

The solutions to this are simple, even if they are not easy. When you get thrown from the Crazy horse, take a breath, clear your thoughts and get back up on the saddle as quickly and gracefully as possible. You have a contract with your partner. Hold his feet to the fire about honoring it. Invite him to do the same with you, and most importantly, you hold your own feet to the fire.

Changing behavior is difficult for everyone, even sane people. Just like smoking, though, it is not impossible for anyone to succeed who is determined enough to make the change.

It is for this reason we suggest you might consider the addiction model as a framework for how handle mistakes, or, "relapses" if you please.

What you may find in many cases is that your partner has become so conditioned and accustomed to Crazy's abuses that it can be rightfully seen as an addictive problem. That can also happen to you. In that light, you and your partner might find it wise to view yourselves as Crazyholics in need of detox and permanent abstinence. Seeing Crazy as a toxic substance, rather than a toxic person, may help make it easier to impersonally set limits and keep them.

What is most helpful about the addiction model is that it gives you a way to track your mistakes, explain them and develop plans to overcome them the next time without the burden of guilt or blame. That last part is critical. If every slip or mistake on your part ends up with you carrying guilt and self-blaming (or blaming your partner) it will quickly sap the motivation for you to get back up on the horse and ride. People want to ride to victory, not a needlessly self-imposed sense of failure.

Treat your mistakes as valuable lessons. Learn from them. Remind yourself that behavioral changes are difficult, that you are not and don't have to be perfect to make this work. All you have to do is remain in charge of your actions, ever putting your next best step forward. Guilt is for people who intentionally do things wrong, not for people who are struggling through fear and hardships to protect their family and peace of mind.

It may even appear cliché, but it is still true. The best way to get back on the horse is to suck it up and mount. In this case, it is literally all you can do. You are better off treating yourself and your partner with kindness during the process.

If you continue to mount that horse, if you continue to define yourself, who you want to be, want you want and don't want, what you will take and what you will not take, then the world, including Crazy, will start to see you in those terms. And the world, including Crazy, will be forced to respect it.

Crazy seldom wastes nearly as much time on people committed to self-care and strong boundaries. There is no payoff for Crazy in healthy people because healthy people say all kinds of bad words, like no, and sometimes even, hell no.

Healthy people don't look for trouble, nor do they tolerate it, nor do they in our experience suffer from it near as much as people who are not acting in a healthy way.

And that is your true challenge. In the end, Crazy is just one person. In your case she is a powerful person who likely has a family court to do her deluded bidding. She is still just one, though. There will be other Crazies in your life. At work, socially and in church. Crazies are literally everywhere. What you will find with the dedicated application of the principles outlined in this book is that Crazies have less and less interest in being around you. We like our Crazy at a serious distance.

Crazy is attracted to the chinks in your armor. When you have few or none, Crazy, like a burglar spotting a high-end security system, will quickly find another target.

To make that happen for yourself, you need not be perfect. All you need to do is be the person that gets back on and rides every time.

Takeaways

- No one can do this perfectly. Expecting yourself or your partner to never make a mistake is unrealistic.

- View Crazy as a toxic substance, not a toxic person.

- Just say no.

- Whenever you falter, be willing to admit it, take responsibility for it and put yourself back on track.

- Crazy avoids people with firm, healthy boundaries, just as she avoids anything else in life that she cannot control.

Chapter 33

Guidelines for Seeking Professional Help

Ridding Crazy from your life can be challenging, to say the least. You and your partner, individually or jointly, may benefit from seeking professional help for a number of issues—overcoming personal obstacles and fears, getting on the same page, working through guilt or grief and how to best support one another through this process.

That being said, not all therapists, counselors and coaches are cut from the same cloth. As we discussed in a previous chapter, there is a tremendous woman and mommy bias in the mental health field. In addition to the female bias, many therapists are enablers of Crazy and will advise you to appease and enable Crazy rather than say goodbye to her. Pastoral counselors are also often woman biased and Crazy enablers.

Therefore, when selecting a psychologist, counselor or coach, you want to be sure that he or she is a good fit for what you and your partner are trying to accomplish. For starters, we recommend avoiding therapists who are gender ideologues. Believe it or not, many mental health professionals who have Internet bios will identify themselves as feminists, so there's no need to call them to ask more questions about goodness of fit.

To help you find the most suitable mental health professional for your needs, we have created a series of questions to ask your potential counselor. Before paying for a full session, ask the therapist if he or she will do a 5-10 minute screening call for you to get a sense of their position on important issues. If the receptionist or the therapist refuses to do this and insists that you come in for a session, find another therapist.

Screening Questions for Mental Health Professionals

- **Do you believe women can be abusive in relationships?** If the therapist says no, is noncommittal or replies that it's highly unlikely, rare or unusual or that abusive women are really victims of "patriarchal oppression," end the call and keep looking.

- **Do you have experience working with people who are abuse victims of women with Borderline Personality Disorder, Narcissistic Personality Disorder and the other Cluster B disorders?** If the counselor says, no, or that people with BPD are usually the victims of abuse, or gets cagy move on to the next therapist on your list. The therapist may ask if Crazy has ever received an official diagnosis. Explain that after years of craziness, verbal attacks, emotional distance, etc., you researched the ex's behavior and believe it meets the criteria.

- **Do you have experience working with men and women who are targets of female perpetrated abuse?** This may or may not be an issue, that is, if the therapist can acknowledge that women can indeed be abusive without attributing it to feminist ideology and "the patriarchy."

- **What do you typically advise men who are being abused by a woman who may have BPD, NPD, HPD and/or sociopathy?** If they avoid the question by explaining that these are severe mental illnesses, and that you have to exercise patience and learn how not to trigger their behaviors, end the call and keep looking. You've most likely found an enabler.

- **Do you encourage clients to keep working on a relationship, no matter how painful and damaging it is to him or her, or do you accept that some relationships can't be repaired because one partner is too damaged or abusive to be in a healthy relationship?** Remember, you're looking for a therapist who will help you say *goodbye* to Crazy, not keep her in your life indefinitely.

- **Do you have experience helping people with similar issues?** You really don't want to work with someone who is still wet behind the ears or that you have to educate.

- **Do you subscribe to feminist theory in psychotherapy?** If the answer is yes, run like hell. If the answer feels evasive, run faster. Fact: Feminist theory in psychotherapy is like Masculinist theory in psychotherapy. Or for that matter Republican or Democrat theory in psychotherapy. None of these things actually exist, except in the distorted mind of the therapist. The human mind is not a playground for political or gender ideology, yet there are "feminist therapists" out there in great abundance. Avoid them. Avoid them all.

- **What is your understanding of men's issues?** Listen carefully to that answer. If they respond with confusion, put them in the rear view mirror quickly. If you hear them utter key phrases like "patriarchy" or recite a list of generalized negatives about men, e.g. control issues, violence, inability to express feelings, inability to commit, etc., they are giving you another good reason to look elsewhere.

That last question is actually more important than you might imagine. If a psychotherapist, when asked about men's issues, only provides what amounts to a list of pejoratives about men, it is a clear indication that they lack empathy for male clients and will either consciously or unconsciously push for things like "radical acceptance" of unacceptable behavior in women.

All of these questions should help eliminate either therapists who just don't get it or therapists who are Crazy apologists and enablers. Even if you find a therapist who gives acceptable answers to these questions, sometimes you just won't "click" with your counselor. Bottom line, you want a professional who understands and has experience with these issues and with whom you feel comfortable. If you don't feel that way after a session or two, it's okay to end treatment and look for another therapist who is a better fit for you.

Other points to consider are the education level of the therapist. Psychologists have a doctorate in psychology (counseling or clinical are the most common) and have at least twice the credit hours and supervised training hours as masters level clinicians. Psychiatrists are medical doctors. Some do talk therapy, but most primarily prescribe psychotropic medications. Social workers are different from psychologists and masters level clinicians with psychology degrees. Both fields are very female centric, and there's good reason for the man-hating social worker stereotype, so proceed with caution.

It should also be noted that the alphabet after someone's name does not assure aptitude or skill, especially given the broader feminist dominance in academia. The indoctrination into propagandized pseudoscience now pervading the humanities and social sciences has resulted in a mental health field that is just crazy about Crazy. She's a cash cow, a political cause and a potential cause célèbre all rolled up into one. Nice work for a Columbia grad who believes that every man on the planet is about to get in touch with his inner rapist.

Not such a good deal for you.

So remember to ensure that your therapist is not as much as a whack job as Crazy. Always remember that you are not talking to a guru or prophet, but a fallible human being just like you. Ask the questions, and if the answers aren't right then prudence is in order.

You should definitely exercise care with faith-based counselors as well. Not all, but many are also female-biased and will blame men who are being abused for not "leading" their families. Good luck leading Crazy! It doesn't work. Coaches are another option, but look into their qualifications. Many have very little education in psychology and human change processes. Coaching is different from therapy in that it has more of a focus on the present, is solution-focused and is more active than traditional therapy.

Takeaways

- Choose a helping professional carefully and wisely. The mental health field is Crazy-biased and many counselors are Crazy enablers and apologists.

- Take a proactive and assertive role in selecting a potential therapist, counselor or coach. Interview them carefully on their beliefs and experience in helping others with similar issues. Consider the importance of your choice.

- It is okay to end treatment at any time with a therapist or coach if you don't think they are a good fit or who isn't helpful.

Chapter 34

Face-to-Face Interactions

We would be remiss if we did not start this chapter with anything less than a first word of advice about having face-to-face time with Crazy. Don't do it.

You may be asking yourself, "But how can I co-parent with Crazy if I don't see her?" or "Won't that make us look like we're being uncooperative to the judge?" or "What if that makes Crazy angry?" or "What's wrong with having live, in person contact with Crazy?"

If you are asking yourselves these questions, you may want to consider going back to the first page of this book and starting all over. Saying goodbye to Crazy means *saying goodbye*. It means you are parallel parenting, not co-parenting. You can't say goodbye to someone who continues to be a physical presence in your lives.

It helps to get this one firmly in place in your mind. We will start with the basics.

There is rarely a legitimate reason to do it.

When all is said and done, the times you really need to be in Crazy's physical proximity are rare and should always be very brief. Any in-person contact with Crazy should be a planned event for you, preferably with you wired and recording at all times. The only thing worse than face time with Crazy is spontaneous face time with Crazy. Unplanned face time with Crazy makes as much sense as vacationing at a leper colony.

Setting this limit with Crazy can take more gumption than she is used to seeing, but if you are creative, even when children are involved, you can often cut physical exposure to Crazy by roughly 100%, which of course is the goal.

Parenting issues, aside from unplanned child emergencies, should be detailed and addressed in your parallel parenting agreement, as discussed earlier. A really effective parenting order will also specify how you handle child emergencies. Remember, the goal is to minimize conflict, and you do that by minimizing contact with Crazy, especially physical contact. All communication should be in writing for the reasons we discussed in the chapter on communicating with Crazy.

It helps you cut your puppet strings and dismantling your buttons.

Crazy is at her best when she has a live audience. It allows her to read your body language and facial expressions that may betray your emotional responses to craziness. In person, Crazy can read protective body postures, flickers of pain, anger and or shame—whatever emotions Crazy is trying to elicit. She can see if the buttons she's pushing and strings she's pulling are working. Crazy is exceptionally skilled at discerning and manipulating emotional states in her targets, so we aim to hold our cards very close to the chest.

It signifies Crazy's place in the pecking order of your lives.

Additionally, as we have noted numerous times, CRAZY DOES NOT LIKE TO BE IGNORED. Even if Crazy has recoupled, she may still push for face time. She still wants to be the central focus in your husband's life, and gosh darn it, *how dare he ignore her? She is The Mother of Their Children!* Reducing physical contact lets Crazy know what her role is in your lives—no role at all.

It greatly reduces her ability to control you.

We know this might sound crazy, but Crazy enjoys bending others to her will. Creating and enforcing boundaries that decrease or eliminate physical contact with Crazy will often incentivize her to push for more contact or try to try to force contact, for instance, by scheduling a bogus hearing with your husband in Family Court.

If Crazy were a seal, face time would be her fresh herring. That drive in her is the engine house for all the damage she has been inflicting so far. Cutting out your face time with Crazy doesn't eliminate all of her power to cause problems, but it is a magnificent and necessary place to start.

Now let's look at the ground rules for face-to-face interactions, that is, if you must have them.

Never enter her home, and do not allow her to enter your home. Ever. That means that you don't go inside to deliver or pick up children. If the kids are old enough, let them come out to the car as you watch, preferably at a pre-arranged neutral spot with good lighting and plenty of foot traffic. Crazy hates witnesses. You will learn to love them.

The exchange of children is not the time for any sort of small talk. Indeed the time for small talk with Crazy has long passed. As previously discussed, any required conversation should be ultra-brief—less than a minute. Anything detailed can be handled via email in advance or later.

This is another good opportunity to consider that if you are managing your communication with Crazy effectively, the only conversation you should require is a civil "hello" for the sake of the children, and "Say goodbye to Mommy," for the same reason.

Say it, then turn and walk, each and every time.

If Crazy attempts to engage you at any point, you say, "Sorry, we have to run. Shoot us an email." Keep walking. Don't look back.

You do not need to attend school meetings with Crazy. Remember, Crazy does not co-parent. That's the reason for parallel parenting. Meetings with teachers and school counselors can be scheduled, depending on the terms of the divorce, without Crazy being there. At school events, be careful to sit far enough away from Crazy to not see or even recognize her. If that is not possible, ignore her completely. Do not make eye contact or respond to any attempt to engage you. And yes, if you have to, leave.

Never be alone with Crazy. This is a deal-breaker. The unfortunate reality is that if your husband is still justifying any alone time at all with Crazy, he is likely not ready to end the chaos she is creating in both of your lives. That may mean some tough decisions for you, but as we have discussed at length, fending off Crazy alone is not going to work.

Be wired like a DEA snitch. As we said, you will learn to love third party witnesses. A concealed audio or video recorder is like your own personal witness who never leaves your side. It is important to check with your attorney to confirm local laws, but in many jurisdictions, there is no presumption to privacy in public places. The law is not so cut-and-dried on private property where an assumption or privacy might be reasonable, but as you are committed to not enter her home or allow her to enter yours that should not be a problem.

Twenty minutes of online shopping should get you everything you need in terms of recording equipment at very reasonable prices.

Say hello to Skype.[27] No, this is not product placement. We don't have a deal with Skype. Skype, however, is a very useful internet based voice communication product when dealing with Crazy because it provides a very affordable way (free) to record phone calls with a product called mp3SkypeRecorder.[28]

Again, we recommend all or most communication with Crazy be in writing. However, we understand that sometimes this just isn't possible. Written communication is preferable for many reasons.

Mostly, it eliminates he said-she said disputes and the issue of the jurisdictional legalities of audio and video recording.

We also strongly recommend that you let all incoming phone calls from Crazy go to voicemail. If there is anything of substance, reply via email. If she leaves a message demanding you call her, but doesn't say why, reply via email asking what she wants to discuss. If she replies saying she wants to speak with you, reply by email that you prefer to communicate in writing. Also, you don't have to worry about legal issues with voicemail and answering machines because if Crazy leaves a message she knows she is being recorded.

If recording phone calls, it is necessary to know if you are in a one-party or two-party state.[29] One-party states only require one person to be aware the call is being recorded. Two-party states require that both parties be aware. When there is one person in a one-party state and one person in a two-party state, then the laws of the two-party state apply.

If the two-party state law applies, we suggest you advise her every time you have phone contact that she is being recorded. If your contact with Crazy is international, consult your attorney. Of course, we remind you that email still reigns supreme in efficiency and efficacy.

Say goodbye to extended family when necessary. Crazy often weaves her way into many family relationships. It is one of her preferred methods of exerting control. It is also how she stays connected to her former in-laws and other extended family members so she can continue to stir up problems and run smear campaigns. Crazy often succeeds at this, especially if his family has similar issues as Crazy or if she has made it clear that they will not see their grandchildren, nieces or nephews if they do not allow her to be the gatekeeper.

The two of you need to be prepared to stand together and draw lines where needed. If Crazy is alienating his children from him and teaching them that you are a home wrecker, even while chumming it up with his parents or siblings, then it is likely time to tell them they have decisions to make. Namely, that you have no intention of maintaining a relationship with those enabling the person who continues to inflict suffering on your family. The same goes for friends.

If you are fortunate enough to have family and friends who might understand, this would be a good time to appeal to them stand with you in solidarity.

We know these are harsh choices. That is Crazy's legacy: damage and harsh choices. Hating those choices is reasonable, but not making them is perilous.

All the messiness Crazy has visited in your life started face-to-face. A great deal of saying goodbye to Crazy is by making sure there is little to none of that in the future, either in person or by proxy with other people who Crazy manipulates and uses.

It is easy to find much of this overwhelming. Recording devices, drawing lines with other family members and friends and developing routines like you see in a spy movie—it can feel like a lot to take on, and in some ways it is. It pays, though, in dividends of peace and freedom from her reach. You will find that once these techniques become part of your standard routine, they are not that time consuming and easily become habits that don't require much effort or thought. In fact, most of them are big time savers.

Less time with Crazy is more time for you and your relationship. You remember that, don't you? It was what you first wanted when you met him.

Crazy's deepest damage is that she is a thief of time. She takes all the time she can and tends to ruin what she cannot take. By moving away from her being the center of attention you can return to the things in life you would be dealing with before she rode in on the Crazy Train.

Ultimately, the goal is to get her out of your mind, not just out of your face.

Takeaways

- Face-to-face interactions with Crazy are to be avoided altogether if at all possible.

- If you must have face time with Crazy, do so in a well-lit, public place with witnesses and a recording device on your person.

- Any necessary face time with Crazy should be known about and planned in advance.

- If you know you are going to be in Crazy's presence have either a third party witness with you or a recording device or both, if possible.

- Do not let Crazy enter your home and do not enter hers for any reason. If Crazy turns up on your doorstep, tell her to leave. If she does not, call the police.

- There is never a good reason to be alone with Crazy, so don't do it.

Chapter 35

Redefining Winning

If you have been going head to head with Crazy for any length of time, you have probably had to readjust concepts like truth, fairness and justice—especially in family court. It may even seem like being a dishonest, conniving, abusive, unemployed or underemployed jerk is how one "wins." It certainly seems like Crazy gets rewarded for being this way, or, at the very least, doesn't experience any meaningful, real-world consequences for behaving this way most of the time.

When it comes to Crazy, there is typically no *winning* in the traditional sense. *Winning* with Crazy is just one more thing you will need to redefine and create for yourselves rather than waiting for Crazy to calm down or for the legal system to help you.

In fact, much of the time, it may look like Crazy succeeds in her efforts to cause you and your loved ones harm and to turn the children against their father and you. It probably also seems like Crazy is frequently aided and abetted by law enforcement, the family court, friends, family, mental health professionals and other negative advocates and flying monkeys in her efforts to cause harm.

Ultimately, there are no winners in Crazy's sick games and scorched-earth tactics to punish your husband for no longer wanting to be abused and controlled by her and to get on with his life with you. It is a zero sum game in which everyone seems to lose—the children, their father, step- and half-siblings, extended family and you. In fact, everyone seems to lose except Crazy and her attorney, both of whom seem happier than a pig in its own refuse with the destruction and chaos she causes. Except that Crazy is rarely happy. In the end, she will go to her grave a bitter "victim." We understand that this offers little comfort to you now.

First, let's understand what winning against Crazy does NOT mean.

Winning does not mean that you will get Crazy to see the light and stop being crazy. This is not going to happen, so quit trying to reason with or explain your positions to Crazy. Doing so just gives her power and the pleasure of seeing you tap dance to her tune. Crazy's interests may sometimes line up with the best interests of the children and you, in which case you may get her to concede. However, that is typically the exception and not the rule. Crazy will often act against her own best interests if she thinks it will cause your husband and you harm. That's just one of the reasons we call Crazy crazy.

Winning does not mean that you will achieve victories in family court against Crazy. Things may go your way from time to time, and we hope they do, but they may not. Sometimes Crazy can have a string of DUI arrests, a breathalyzer connected to her car ignition that she dismantles, a YouTube channel's worth of crazy, abusive audio recordings and a host of other evidence demonstrating just how unfit of a parent she is, and she will still retain custody. She willfully disobeys court orders and judges will barely give her a slap on the wrist. Do not look to the legal system in order to win against Crazy. More and more it seems like family court is a system by sociopaths for sociopaths.

Winning against Crazy does not necessarily mean you will be able to heal alienated children and repair your relationship with them. Again, we hope you do, but you may not—especially if your family court does not assist you in getting you and the children the help you need. The relationship with your children may be damaged irrevocably. This is just one of the harsh realities of Crazy.

Winning against Crazy does not mean that you will be able to persuade friends, family, teachers, mental health professionals, and the like that Crazy really is the demented fruit bat that she is. If she is "high-functioning" (i.e., has enough self-control to keep the super mom/saint act going in public), there are some people who will never believe the truth about her until or unless she personally harms them. You may lose important relationships or be viewed as a social pariah. You might have to develop an entirely new circle of friends or even change jobs if Crazy is able to infiltrate your workplace and turn your colleagues against you. Heck, your husband's own family might even side with Crazy.

Now that we know what winning against Crazy does not mean, let's look at what winning means to Crazy.

For Crazy, *winning* means she has the ability to hurt you and your husband. It means she has the ability to intrude upon and disrupt your lives, to cause you social harm, to cause you financial harm and to cause you legal harm. Winning for Crazy means she gets to destroy or take away things and people she thinks are important to your husband and you. A win for Crazy is forcing you, or getting the courts to force you, to do something you don't want to do. If she could, Crazy would take a bath in yours and your husband's tears. Your pain brings her pleasure.

There is no *winning* in the traditional sense against this kind of gleeful sadism.

The win for you is removing Crazy and her minions from your lives as best you can and nurturing and cherishing what is good in your lives. The win is reducing Crazy and her ability to screw with you to the tiniest, infinitesimal speck of insignificance in your lives.

In order to win against Crazy, you need to accept certain truths and develop new mindsets. You must come to terms with, accept and practice the following:

- **Boundaries are GOOD.** We discuss the importance of boundaries in *chapter 26* . Boundaries are your first line of defense against Crazy. Without boundaries, you're screwed. Discover the joy of saying NO. Discover the joy of low or no contact. Boundaries are your deflector shield. You are not being mean or controlling by having enforceable boundaries, despite whatever Crazy says to the contrary. Having boundaries is healthy and necessary.

- **The normal rules of civility do not apply to Crazy.** Crazy counts on people being too nice to call her on her crap. Crazy banks on people's dislike of confrontation to get away with her shenanigans. If you're going to file a contempt order against Crazy, don't give her a heads up. Don't warn her that you're going to deliver a consequence, just deliver the consequence when she violates a boundary or a court order. You are not honor bound to treat Crazy as if she isn't Crazy.

- **Crazy is going to continue being crazy.** Crazy is not going to undergo a miraculous personality metamorphosis and become a rational, reasonable human being, so plan and act accordingly. If there is a wrong choice, Crazy is going to make it. If there is a way for Crazy to cause problems, she is going to do it. In practical terms, this means keep your life— your triumphs and your struggles—private. Don't broadcast information on social media that will trigger jealousy or help her find new ways to harm you.

- **You cannot protect Crazy and protect yourselves at the same time.** This is a tough one. Frequently, men do not want The Mother of Their Children to experience consequences like going to jail if, for example, Crazy hits them, steals money from them, etc. Having a sense of chivalry towards Crazy, especially when Crazy is hell-bent on destruction, is seriously misguided. If Crazy wants to hang herself with her own rope, *let her*. Do not intervene. Do not get in her way. Stand back and document it. At some point, hopefully, you'll have enough documentation for the family courts to actually do something about it.

- **Crazy wants to cause you harm no matter what you do, so always do what's good for you.** Many men and women do not protect themselves from Crazy by enforcing boundaries and implementing consequences because they fear Crazy will become angry (more like angrier) and retaliate. Crazy is going to be angry and do things to hurt you no matter what you do, so act in your best interests and the best interests of the children. Crazy is not going to stop messing with you until she experiences enough adverse consequences for continuing to do so. Will she retaliate? Probably. And when she does, you enforce another consequence and another and another and another for her retaliations until she stops or ends up in jail. Whichever comes first.

- **Crazy has neither compassion nor empathy.** Master your emotional reactions. Do not let Crazy know when she has hurt you or when she gets to you. Reacting to Crazy gives her a roadmap to what buttons to push. If boundaries are the wall around your fortress, then gaining control over your emotional responses to Crazy, or at least learning how to mask them, is the moat. It's no fun for Crazy if she doesn't get to hear you say, "Ouch!" If you can't make it painful for Crazy to continue to mess with you, then make it boring.

Winning against Crazy is almost entirely under your control. If you can develop these mindsets and practices, you *can* greatly reduce in any meaningful capacity or, if no children are involved, totally eradicate her presence in your life. When you understand that Crazy's emails, texts and other communications are meant to be inflammatory and to upset you, you disempower Crazy. And what kind of power is that really? The power to piss people off? If Crazy doesn't have that, what does she have?

You get to decide what you will and will not allow to upset you, so don't let her. Allowing Crazy to get to you is kind of like letting a mouthy 13-year old get under your skin. Ignore her and laugh it off with your husband. That's the 24-carat win.

You and your husband win when you no longer jump whenever Crazy yanks your chain. When you start reeling that chain in to make it more difficult and fruitless for her to yank it in the first place, you win. You win when Crazy no longer takes up real estate in your marriage, in your daily conversations or in your head. You win when you drop the rope and no longer participate in her never-ending rounds of tug-of-war or keep-away with the children.

You win when you start to enjoy life's daily pleasures again—a pleasant family dinner, a walk with your husband, a promotion, your son winning the spelling bee, birthdays—everyday life. You win when you read one of Crazy's crazy emails, roll your eyes and think, "Oh look, Crazy's being crazy again. Whatever."

Crazy knows how to get a rise out of your husband and you. She figured that out a long time ago. This means that in addition to disengaging and practicing emotional detachment with Crazy, you may also need to let go of other important things and relationships. We understand this is not easy—particularly if some of the relationships you need to step back from are with your children and other loved ones. Ultimately, you have to decide what it's worth to you to say goodbye to Crazy.

And there's the rub. It is what our work, this book and your challenge all boil down to. Saying goodbye to Crazy, like all forms of peace and happiness, is a 100% inside job. It is a challenge that will literally define your life, who you are as a person and who you are as a couple.

Saying goodbye to Crazy is not just about putting the kibosh on a single defective cuckoo. It is a conscious decision to live comfortably in your own skin, by your own rules and values. It is, in the truest sense, about whether you live your life or surrender it to others who would do you harm.

These are things that can only be accomplished by you and those who stand with you.

Takeaways

- Saying goodbye to Crazy is really about saying hello to running your own life on your own terms.

- It is you who must decide if the approval of others is worth a life spent mired in fear, anxiety and perpetual conflict—for yourself, for your partner and for your children.

- The war only looks like it is with Crazy. It is actually being waged in your own heart and mind. Take good care of them.

References

1   Kübler-Ross, E. S., (1969). *On death and dying.* Scribner.

2   Freyd, J.J. (1997) Violations of power, adaptive blindness, and betrayal trauma theory. *Feminism & Psychology*, 7, 22-32.

3   Palmatier, T. J. (2011). *Presto, Change-O, DARVO!* *http://www.shrink4men.com/2011/01/19/presto-change-o-darvo-deny-attack-and-reverse-victim-and-offender/*

4   Twenge, J. and Campbell, K.W. (2010). *The Narcissism Epidemic: Living in the Age of Entitlement.* Free Press.

5   Palmatier, T.J. (2011). *Hostile dependency: Is your wife, girlfriend or ex a child masquerading in the body of a woman?* *http://www.shrink4men.com/2011/06/07/hostile-dependency-is-your-wife-girlfriend-or-ex-a-child-masquerading-in-the-body-of-a-woman/*

6   Palmatier, T. J. (2012). *Winning vs. taking: What does winning mean to abusive, high-conflict and/or personality disordered women?* *http://www.shrink4men.com/2012/06/06/winning-vs-taking-what-does-winning-mean-to-abusive-high-conflict-andor-personality-disordered-women/*

7   Schumacher, T.J. *Dealing with control freaks.* *http://www.ec-online.net/knowledge/Articles/control.html*

8   Palmatier, T. J. (2010). Why some high-conflict women kill. *http://shrink4men.com/2010/11/10/why-some-high-conflict-personality-women-kill/*

9   Buchanan, C. M. & Heiges, K. L. (2001). When conflict continues after the divorce ends: Effects of post-divorce conflict on children. In J. Grych and F. Fincham (eds.), Interparental

conflict and child development (pp. 337-362). New York: Cambridge University Press.

10 Gaulier, B., Margerum, J., Price, J. A., & Windell, J. (2007). Defusing the high-conflict divorce: A treatment guide for working with angry couples. Atascadero, CA: Impact Publishers.

11 Brownstone, H. (2009). Tug of war: A judge's verdict on separation, custody battles, and the bitter realities of family court. Ontario, Canada: ECW Press, p. 4.

12 Eddy, W. A. (2005). High-conflict people in legal disputes. USA: Janis Publications.

13 Eddy, W. A. (2004). Splitting: Protecting yourself while divorcing a Borderline or narcissist. Milwaukee, WI: Eggshells Press.

14 Wakefield, H. & Underwager, R. (1990). Personality characteristics of parents making false allegations of sexual abuse in custody disputes. Presented at the Sixth Annual Symposium in Forensic Psychology in Las Vegas, Nevada on March 13, 1990, at the Second Annual Convention of the American Psychological Society in Dallas, Texas, on June 9, 1990, and at the 98th Annual Convention of the American Psychological Association in Boston, Massachusetts, on August 14, 1990.

15 Palmatier, T. J. (2011). Welcome to the land of emotional reasoning: I'd turn back if I were you. Shrink4Men.com: *http://www.shrink4men.com/2011/08/29/welcome-to-the-land-of-emotional-reasoning-id-turn-back-if-i-were-you/.*

16 Eddy, W. A. (2005). High-conflict people in legal disputes. USA: Janis Publications.

17 Palmatier, T. J. (2011). Narcissistic personality disorder and histrionic personality disorder to be eliminated from the DSM-V: Starbucks diagnostics 101.

http://shrink4men.com/2010/12/01/narcissistic-personality-disorder-and-histrionic-personality-disorder-to-be-eliminated-in-the-dsm-v-welcome-to-starbucks-diagnostics/

18 Gardner, R. (1982). *Family evaluations in child custody litigation.* New Jersey: Creative Therapeutics.

19 Clawar, S. S., & Rivlin, B. V. (1991). *Children held hostage: Dealing with programmed and brainwashed children.* Chicago, IL: American Bar Association.

20 Prochaska, J. O., & Norcross, J. C. (2002). Stages of change. In J. C. Norcross (Ed.), Psychotherapy relationships that work (303-313). New York: Oxford University Press.

21 Stahl, P.M. (2000). Parenting after divorce. Impact Publishers.

22 Kelly, J. & Johnston, J. (2001). The alienated child: A reformulation of parental alienation syndrome. *Family & Conciliation Courts Review.* 38, (3), 249-266.

23 Olsen, B.D. (2010). The need for parallel parenting. *www.highconflict.net*

24 Arizona Supreme Court. (2009). Planning for parenting time: Arizona's guide for parents living apart.

25 **OurFamilyWizard.com:** "The OFW™ website reduces divorce conflict between you and the other parent by providing a shared tool for scheduling parenting time calendars and visitation schedules, sharing information and managing expenses like un-reimbursed medical bills.

26 Pedro-Carroll, J. L. (2010). Putting children first: Proven parenting strategies for helping children thrive through divorce. The Penguin Group: New York, NY.

27 *http://www.skype.com/en/*

28 *http://download.cnet.com/MP3-Skype-Recorder/3000-2349_4-75445962.html*

29 *http://www.vegress.com/index.php/can-i-record-calls-in-my-state*

63038007R00146

Made in the USA
Lexington, KY
25 April 2017